Fostering
EMOTIONAL INTELLIGENCE
in K–8 Students

Gwen Doty

Fostering
EMOTIONAL INTELLIGENCE
in K–8 Students

Simple Strategies and Ready-to-Use Activities

CORWIN PRESS, INC.
A Sage Publications Company
Thousand Oaks, California

For information:

Corwin Press, Inc.
A Sage Publications Company
2455 Teller Road
Thousand Oaks, California 91320
E-mail: order@corwinpress.com

Sage Publications Ltd.
6 Bonhill Street
London EC2A 4PU
United Kingdom

Sage Publications India Pvt. Ltd.
M-32 Market
Greater Kailash I
New Delhi 110 048 India

Printed in the United States of America

Library of Congress Cataloging-in-Publication Data

Doty, Gwen.
    Fostering emotional intelligence in K-8 students: Simple strategies and ready-to-use activities / by Gwen Doty.
        p.   cm.
    Includes bibliographical references and index.
    ISBN 0-7619-7747-3 (cloth) — ISBN 0-7619-7748-1 (pbk.)
    1. Affective education-United States.   2. Emotional intelligence.
3. Education, Elementary-Activity programs—United States.
    I. Title.
    LB1072 .D68   2001
    372.13—dc21   00-012961

This book is printed on acid-free paper.

01 02 03 04 05 06 07 7 6 5 4 3 2 1

Acquiring Editor:	Rachel Livsey
Corwin Editorial Assistant:	Phyllis Cappello
Production Editor:	Diane S. Foster
Editorial Assistant:	Cindy Bear
Typesetter/Designer:	Lynn Miyata/Larry K. Bramble
Cover Designer:	Michael Dubowe

Contents

PART III

Incorporating Emotional Intelligence Into the Curriculum   125

Preface

Nathan walked into my classroom, his weak leg dragging, his bald head partially concealed with a baseball cap. His crooked smile and sparkling eyes showed curiosity and trust. I instantly fell in love.

Nathan had many physical problems, as well as academic challenges. Although he was in my sixth-grade class, his records showed his reading and math abilities were on a kindergarten level. As the school year began, I grew increasingly concerned about the skills this boy would need to become a self-sufficient member of society. How would he ever have a prayer of getting a job someday with his low academic abilities?

Slowly, I began to notice some social and emotional strengths in Nathan that didn't match his academic performance. The other students loved him and welcomed him in their cooperative groups. When another student was sad, Nathan often picked up on the child's emotions before the rest of us did. He began coming up to me to tell me when he saw that someone was "feeling bad." And Nathan was amazingly astute regarding his own feelings. He not only understood his own emotions, such as hurt, anger, love, and jealousy, but he could verbalize them to me.

When I read Daniel Goleman's book, *Emotional Intelligence,* I realized Nathan truly had a gift. Even though he was low functioning in a multitude of areas, Nathan was very perceptive when it came to recognizing human emotion. He had the ability to read the feelings of others and had insight into his own inner feelings and emotions. He was able to see the positive side of situations and promote an optimistic point of view. Other students recognized this strength and loved him for it.

Perhaps Nathan was genetically endowed at birth with this sweet and insightful disposition. Perhaps. But when I met his mother, and I saw her warmth and encouragement as she interacted with Nathan,

I decided that she had "taught" Nathan to be emotionally intelligent. I believe, as Goleman does, that people can be taught to become more emotionally intelligent, which enables them to become more successful in life. I believe that we, as teachers, can instill in our students the ability to be emotionally self-aware, insightful regarding the motivations of others, more able to cope with emotional dilemmas in life, and more empathetic and sympathetic of peers. Students would benefit from learning emotional intelligence because they would become more socially adept and able to effectively solve problems, resolve conflicts, and excel in teamwork activities.

These are the very skills businesses are seeking as our young graduates enter the world of work. Emotional intelligence creates individuals who are "people-smart"; individuals who can read other people, who can take on the role of leader as well as the role of facilitator and team member. A quote from Aristotle used by Goleman sums it up. Emotional intelligence creates people who know how "to be angry with the right person, to the right degree, at the right time, for the right purpose, and in the right way." Emotional intelligence creates good decision makers and strong empathizers who have a solid sense of fairness and integrity. That's what emotional intelligence is all about.

Acknowledgments

Throughout my 20 years as a teacher, I continuously searched for inspiration in developing strategies for the diverse learners in my classroom. With such a vast range of social, emotional, behavioral, and academic levels represented in a class of 30 students, how was one teacher supposed to raise these four attributes in each individual?

Because of these concerns, Howard Gardner became an instant hero in my life when he revealed the seven (now eight) multiple intelligences. At once, my educational philosophies and covert beliefs were validated. My style of teaching, which had always made sense to me, was now grounded in research.

Daniel Goleman, author of *Emotional Intelligence,* became my second idol. He explains that emotional intelligence includes self-control, zeal, persistence, and the ability to motivate oneself—all attributes that make a student successful. Emotional intelligence, once developed, can create the avenue for a productive, rewarding, and fulfilling life.

My plan, based on the work of these two gentlemen, was to write a book based on their findings that would demonstrate the benefits and rewards of enriching the curriculum by integrating the concept of emotional intelligence into our content activities. I want to express sincere gratitude to these researchers and authors who gave me the foundation from which I can further explore the concept of student success through emotional intelligence.

The contributions of the following reviewers are gratefully acknowledged.

Ann Marie Smith
Associate Professor
Northern Virginia Community College
Woodbridge, Virginia

Anita Perry
Title I Teacher
Southeast School
Leominster, Massachusetts

Genet Kozik-Rosabal
Assistant Professor
University of Colorado at Boulder
School of Education
Boulder, Colorado

Dr. Tim Green
Assistant Professor of Elementary Education
California State University, Fullerton
Fullerton, California

Ron Wahlen
Technology Coordinator
Conn Global Communications Magnet
Raleigh, North Carolina

Dr. Patrick Akos
School Counselor
Louisa County Middle School
Mineral, Virginia

Virginia Doolittle
Assistant Professor
Rowan University
Glassboro, New Jersey

About the Author

GWEN DOTY, a 20-year veteran in the field of education, has gone beyond the walls of the classroom setting. Throughout her career, she has been involved in curriculum development, assessment, and promotional activities for public education. After receiving a master's degree in oral communication, Gwen began writing materials and training teachers and parents in the most effective methods of communicating with students, whether for academic, social, or emotional purposes. Her passion became one of developing academic, social, and emotional attributes within students through the use of relevant learning, multiple intelligences, and verbal expression. Ms. Doty has conducted numerous educational seminars throughout the United States with the goal of inspiring teachers to connect with their students by integrating emotional and social components into academic lessons. By helping students to understand their feelings, actions, and interests, she believes we are not only helping them gain confidence in their academic endeavors, but we are also giving them the framework for finding a path to their futures.

PART I

Is Emotional Intelligence Just One More Thing We Have to Teach?

1

Understanding Emotional Intelligence

Emotions are not a form of thought, not an additional way to think, not a special cognitive bonus, BUT are fundamental to thought.

— David Gelernter, Computer Scientist

School budgets become tighter across the country, resulting in diminishing numbers of school counselors and self-esteem programs. As our society evolves and parents work longer hours, students often find themselves with a lack of clear direction and unsupervised time on their hands. Teachers see violence and poor self-concepts on the increase in our schools. We are all in agreement that young people in the United States need more avenues to develop wholesome attitudes and make appropriate life decisions. But exactly what we should do to foster positive self-esteem, social skills, and problem-solving abilities remains a bit of a mystery.

As educators, we have been trained to teach academics so that our students reach a point of formal achievement. Our assumption is that once students have mastered the curriculum, they will be on their way to success. But in light of the societal problems just described, we are beginning to realize that we must incorporate programs that enable our students to learn to cope, understand their own value, gain empathy for others, and manage and control their emotions. These factors of emotion, this insight into oneself as well as into the emotions of others, constitute the first steps in gaining essential skills for a successful life.

Rather than shake our heads and wonder what this world is coming to or marvel at how our youth could possibly be driven to a state of mind that would allow violence to prevail, we must take positive action within the walls of the classroom. We must instill within our students the life skills and coping mechanisms to foster appropriate reaction behavior, solid decision-making skills, and principles of honesty that may not be taught elsewhere. Children's lack of training in handling anger, hurt, and grief reveals the true problem, and their inappropriate responses to these emotions can lead to the violent acts we now witness in our schools.

Why are we seeing a tremendous increase in aggressive and destructive behavior among our students? Research suggests that the trait of aggression in children often results when they have been severely neglected or abused, similar to when an animal that has been tortured becomes aggressive. When animals and humans are raised among violent adults, they develop a similar aggressive behavior pattern. When children aren't equipped with effective problem-solving skills, good communication/negotiation techniques, and positive role modeling, or when children consistently feel frustrated from a "lack" of something (such as nurturing), the result is a high degree of aggression. With parents working away from home, children left alone without adult interaction, and our society as a whole tolerating more violence, teachers are becoming increasingly concerned about children using hostile avenues to solve their problems.

As we observe students in the classroom, we see two primary responses to social interaction—aggression and cooperation. Both of these behaviors are means of managing conflict and establishing peer relationships. Aggressive students see that they can obtain their desired results by bullying or causing harm to other children. For example, during a class baseball game, a student, angry that he's not getting to play his fair share, pushes to the front of the batting line in an effort to get more chances at the plate. This child has established a role of leader rather than follower and has received the bonus of more playing time. Without any guidance or training, an aggressive pattern is established.

This incident is an opportune "teachable moment." The school setting offers the ideal conditions to foster appropriate responses to this student's emotions. As teachers, we have opportunities to interact with students, modeling positive and appropriate emotional responses for our students. We can share our own honest feelings and verbalize our responses as we solve dilemmas.

An abundance of research demonstrates that the implementation of emotional literacy classes truly does increase student coping skills as well as academic achievement (Goleman, 1997). Specifically, teaching students the skills outlined in this book have had the following overall effects (Branden, 1994; Goleman, 1997; Slovey & Mayer, 1990):

Awareness of Self and Others

- Better ability to recognize and name own emotions
- Better ability to understand the causes for feelings
- Better ability to distinguish between feelings and actions

Approval of Self and Others

- More positive feelings about self, school, and family
- Better ability to handle stress
- Less social anxiety and loneliness
- Better ability to see another's perspective
- Improved empathy with others

Mastering Self-Responsibility

- Better equipped with anger management tools
- Fewer class disruptions, fights, put-downs, and so on
- Better ability to express anger appropriately
- Less aggressive and self-destructive behavior

Finding Personal Meaning

- Better ability to analyze and understand relationships
- Better ability to solve problems in relationships
- More assertive and skilled with communication

Valuing Honesty and Ethics

- Increased friendliness and involvement with peers
- More considerate of peers
- Increased group interaction skills

- More sharing and helpfulness evident

- More democratic in dealing with others

Is emotional intelligence just one more thing we have to teach? Absolutely not. Emotional intelligence is not a subject or an isolated skill that can be taught. It is the process of learning to understand our own emotions, learning to understand the emotions of others, gaining proficiency in positive emotional responses in oneself, and recognizing and accepting the emotional responses of others. The teacher's role in this learning process is to act as facilitator and role model to enhance student understanding of emotional intelligence. Integrating emotional intelligence into content areas should not be difficult, especially in language arts and social studies. Integration could be as simple as asking students to write a reflection paragraph about what they think the character in the story should do to solve the problem. This type of reflective writing can result in stimulating and productive classroom discussions about appropriate responses to an emotional situation.

Through relevant teaching and meaningful learning, we can help students gain insight into their own emotional intelligence. Students learn to actually increase their levels of emotional understanding. Benefits could include higher academic performance, improved social skills, less school violence, and a greater sense of self-worth.

Emotional intelligence, or EI, can be observed through the appearance, gestures, and actions of students. By referring to Table 1.1, teachers can begin to make mental notes of students who appear to have EI strengths and of those who would benefit from EI training.

TABLE 1.1 What Does Emotional Intelligence Look Like?

High Emotional Intelligence	*Low Emotional Intelligence*
Uses "I" messages	Makes blame statements
Can openly express feelings	Cannot share feelings verbally
Isn't preoccupied with negative emotions	Lets negative feelings dominate
Reads nonverbal language effectively	Is oblivious to nonverbal communication
Makes decisions based on feelings and logic	Acts without reasoning or logic
Accepts self and others	Is not accepting of self or others
Can apply self-responsibility	Has not learned to accept responsibility
Can communicate assertively	Uses passive or aggressive communication
Is motivated by personal meaning	Is motivated by rewards and instant gratification
Is emotionally resilient	Carries grudges; is unforgiving
Promotes the optimistic point of view	Focuses on the negative point of view
Can identify the feelings of others	Is not perceptive of the feelings of others
Doesn't blame others for mistakes	Feels it is always someone else's fault
Says, "I feel . . ."	Says, "YOU always . . ."
Reacts to hurt by processing feelings	Reacts to hurt with physical violence
Reacts to grief by sharing feelings	Reacts to grief by stifling emotions
Usually feels respected and competent	Usually feels inadequate and defensive
Is a good listener	Is a poor listener
Talks out problems or miscommunications	Acts out when there is a problem

2

Integrating Emotional Intelligence With Academic Skills

When wondering if academic intelligence and emotional intelligence are a natural fit, consider this: During a brain operation, if your emotional connections are severed, you cannot make even the most simple decision afterward. Why? Because as a result of severing the part of the brain that controls emotions from the rest of the brain, you don't know how you will feel about the choices you make (Sperry, 1974).

Our emotions can serve as a built-in guidance system, alerting us when we have a need that isn't being met. These needs can be emotional, such as the needs for acceptance, nurturing, and love. Or they can be academic, such as the need for a different teaching tactic or an alternative assignment based on intelligence strengths or weakness. Emotions, when combined with reason, logic, and academic skill, create a powerful tool for student success.

Instilling emotional and academic learning within students is the ultimate achievement of a teacher. But how would that work? How do the learning processes of these two intelligences tie together, and how does a teacher design lessons that foster both emotional and intellectual learning?

In a classroom that fosters the integration of academic and emotional learning, the first step is to create a classroom environment that feels caring, open, and positive. Students can help facilitate this environment by creating a "No Fear" plan. In a No Fear plan, students determine what they need to feel safe and secure in the classroom. No Fear rules might include the following suggestions:

- Safety—Students will be free from physical violence or bullying and from emotional pain such as threats, manipulation, embarrassment, or stress.

- Choices—Students will have real choices in academic and emotional learning.

- Respect—Students will show respect for their own feelings and for those of others.

- Multiple intelligences—Students will be aware of the individual intellectual strengths of others and will nurture and support these various abilities.

- Motivation—Students will engage in activities they find exciting and stimulating.

- Relevant learning—Students will be provided with lessons in which they can find personally meaningful connections to the "real world."

- Emotional intelligence—Students will value, discuss, and validate their own feelings and those of others.

Once the classroom atmosphere has been established, teachers need to formulate a new and revised definition of "learning" for themselves as well as for the students. The creation of the learning definition should occur through cooperative classroom discussion to make sure everyone "buys into" the final decision. For clarity, we can use the following definition that incorporates academic and emotional learning:

Learning is the combined collection of acquired knowledge, the understanding of skills, tendencies toward dispositions, and the emotional state during these processes (Katz, 1985, pp. 1-2).

According to author and researcher Lilian G. Katz (1985, pp. 1-2), learning can be divided into four categories:

Knowledge. In the elementary years children begin to acquire knowledge. Knowledge consists of facts, ideas, concepts, vocabulary, and stories. Children acquire knowledge by listening to answers to their questions and through explanations, descriptions, observations.

Skills. Using their knowledge, students begin to acquire skills. Skills are small units of action that occur in a short time. They are easily observed or inferred. Adding and subtracting, drawing, and verbal and written communication are examples of skills taught in schools.

Dispositions. Dispositions are habits of mind or tendencies to respond to certain situations in certain ways. Being curious, friendly, timid, bossy, or creative are disposition attributes rather than skills or pieces of knowledge. One may have a disposition to be an artist, but without the skills to go with that disposition, the result may be less than successful.

Feelings. Feelings are learned emotional states, such as feelings of competence, of belonging, of love, and of tolerance or intolerance toward others.

Using these four learning attributes as a model, how do we make the curriculum connection between emotional and academic intelligence? When a student has gained *knowledge* and *skills,* we could say that this student has become proficient in *surface knowledge.* Surface knowledge results when an individual has programmed or memorized the mechanics of any subject (Caine & Caine, 1994). But this student may not necessarily have a disposition toward the learned information or any kind of "felt meaning" for the information. Unfortunately, there are many classrooms full of students who are never given opportunities to expand and build on that surface knowledge to increase its personal meaning. Teachers who provide lesson strategies that include meaningful connections, reflective opportunities, and specific feedback regarding content and feelings, are teaching students how to gain natural knowledge—or a deeper, more meaningful knowledge that transfers to long-term memory (see Figure 2.1). In addition, when students are actively involved in learning, they find personal meaning in the assignments, and through reflection they gain insight into their feelings and are more apt to find emotional and academic success.

Using the diagram in Figure 2.2, make note of the characteristics of both academic and emotional intelligence. Imagine students with *only* academic intelligence. These students might demonstrate excellent written and verbal skills, be able to articulate numbers, and have a thorough understanding of the scientific process. But with-

FIGURE 2.1. Steps to Achieving Academic and Emotional Intelligence

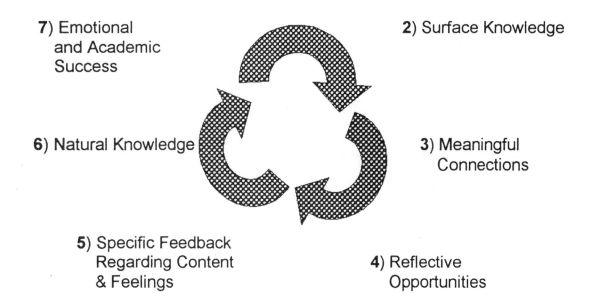

out emotional intelligence, they would never be able to attach any real feelings or emotions to this learning. Without an understanding of themselves and without an awareness of others, this knowledge would seem very empty and hollow. For true meaning and insight to occur, there must be a connection between knowledge/skills learning and disposition/feelings learning. This connection enables learners not only to recognize deep and personal meanings in the knowledge, but it also raises their feelings of self-worth because they have gained insight and understanding of the material.

In designing lessons involving emotional training, use the checklist in Figure 2.3. This may help narrow the specific areas to incorporate into your content lessons. During a given week, use tally marks to show the number of students who have performed a behavioral response, such as bullying. At the end of the week, if you notice that five or more checkmarks are listed alongside a particular behavioral response, you have an indication of an area that needs to be addressed during your integration of academic and emotional activities.

Use the sample planning sheet in Figure 2.4 as you begin the integration of academic and emotional learning strategies.

FIGURE 2.2. Characteristics of Academic and Emotional Intelligence

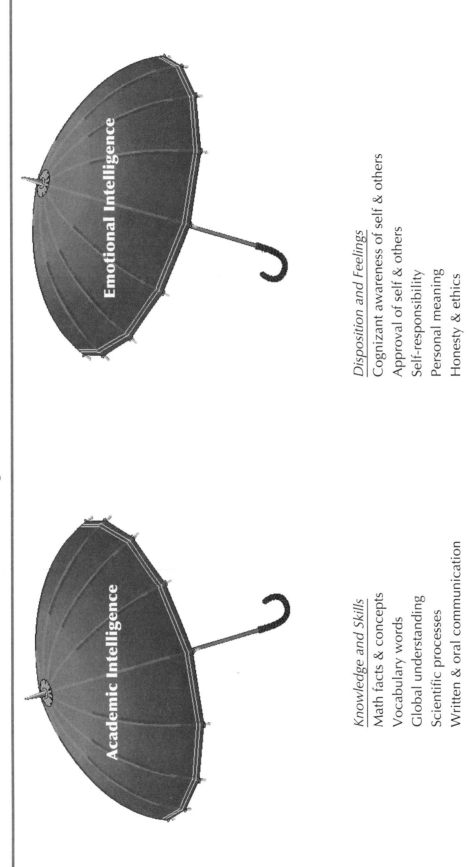

Knowledge and Skills
Math facts & concepts
Vocabulary words
Global understanding
Scientific processes
Written & oral communication

Disposition and Feelings
Cognizant awareness of self & others
Approval of self & others
Self-responsibility
Personal meaning
Honesty & ethics

NOTE: The skills and knowledge of academic intelligence in conjunction with positive disposition and feelings can make a powerful recipe for success.

FIGURE 2.3. Emotional Intelligence Training Needs Checklist

☐ Bullying   ☐ Obscene language

☐ Panicking   ☐ Fighting

☐ Attacking   ☐ Pushing

☐ Teasing   ☐ Stealing

☐ Interrupting   ☐ Withdrawing

☐ Belligerence   ☐ Cheating

☐ Disrespect   ☐ Poor decision making

☐ Verbal threats   ☐ Instigating/agitating

☐ Physical threats   ☐ Poor impulse control

☐ Inappropriate physical responses   ☐ Attention seeking through misbehavior

NOTE: Using this checklist to identify recurring behavioral responses, you can determine which areas of emotional intelligence training you need to immediately incorporate into your content lessons. The sample planning sheet in Figure 2.4 may assist you as you begin the integration of academic and emotional learning strategies.

FIGURE 2.4. Sample Planning Sheet

Subject	Lesson Objective	Emotional Intelligence Benefits
Reading	Cause and effect	The teacher reads various passages from well-known stories. Students determine the cause and effect. The class discusses how the characters could have solved their problems in more appropriate ways.
Writing	Personal narrative	During an essay writing, students have the opportunity to share a time in their lives when they reacted appropriately in a bad situation.
Social Studies	Understanding the Confederate point of view in the Civil War	In cooperative groups, students discuss the feelings and emotions of the Confederate soldiers.
Health	Smoking cessation	A class discussion in which students are given the chance to discuss the loss of a loved one because of conditions resulting from tobacco use.

Learning Frameworks for Integration

Certain curriculum frameworks, such as those that follow, lend themselves more easily to combining academic learning with emotional learning. If you are currently using these structures, it should be very easy to add the emotional intelligence component to each lesson.

Thematic Learning

In the thematic learning structure, the teacher (or perhaps the class) decides on a particular "big idea" theme to study. All of the content lessons, centers, and free-time activities revolve around the theme. The subjects of language arts, math, science, and social studies are all related to that theme. In schools where students have different teachers for different content areas, those teachers work together to use the same theme. A Revolutionary War theme sample is provided in Figure 2.5.

FIGURE 2.5. Sample Theme: Revolutionary War

Subject	Lesson Objective	Emotional Intelligence Integration
Reading/ Language Arts	Students compare and contrast colonist and British points of view with a Venn Diagram.	Students share Venn Diagram results orally and discuss what actions the colonists took based on their strong feelings.
Math	Students chart battles and casualties.	Based on numbers of casualties, was freedom worth the price they paid? Students discuss this.
Writing/ Language Arts	Students write a letter to a relative in England.	Students explain their feelings and actions as colonists who want freedom from England.
Science	Students collect data to determine who actually fired the first shot at Lexington.	Students discuss the question, Were there alternatives to this issue other than war?

Project Learning

Project learning involves a collection of elements that students complete for a final project. This culminating project displays between 5 and 10 components demonstrating the students' mastery of content skills (academic intelligence) as well as their disposition and feelings (emotional intelligence). An example of a project is shown in Exhibit 2.1.

By including assignments that require student input, thought, and reflective responses, the content becomes more personally relevant to the learner. According to Exhibit 2.1, students who participated in this project gained a deeper understanding of the harmful effects of tobacco use and had opportunities to contemplate their own convictions about tobacco. Classroom discussions took place concerning the cause-and-effect benefits and drawbacks of tobacco use. Students were also able to reflect on and discuss the long-term effects of tobacco. Students wrote in journals about their decisions regarding tobacco use. In summary, the academic process was tied to emotional learning, resulting in student success and feelings of adequacy.

Problem-Based Learning

In this learning structure, the teacher provides students with an authentic and relevant problem that is also tied to the current topic

⚙ EXHIBIT 2.1. Tobacco Awareness Project

Components

✓ Chart showing percentages of American deaths due to tobacco

✓ Poem about benefits of being tobacco-free

✓ Illustration of the respiratory system and effects of tobacco on it

✓ Student "Health Diary" with reflections and feelings about personal experiences (self or acquaintance) regarding tobacco

✓ Student survey results of classmate feelings about tobacco use

---

being studied. The unit begins with an unstructured, open-ended problem such as the local pond pollution. Students become involved in the steps of problem solving, investigative processes, formulating hypotheses, testing their solutions, and forming new plans if test results are not successful. To begin, you might want students in cooperative groups to fill in a problem-solving sheet as they begin their thinking processes regarding possible solutions to this pollution problem.

Pollution Solutions

State the problem: _____

_____

Brainstorm (all possible thoughts): _____

_____

_____

Narrow to three best options: _____

_____

_____

Final best solution: _____

_____

Students work in teams using the particular solution of their choice to try to solve the problem at hand. At the conclusion of the unit, when students have "solved" their problem, they again become involved with reflective processing to ensure their deep understanding of the material and to provide opportunities for self-acceptance, self-worth, and acceptance of peers and their worth.

A typical reflection page at the end of a problem-based unit might include the following questions:

- What problem were you and your teammates trying to solve?

- Describe the solution method that you and your teammates decided to test.

- Describe the methods and results of your test.

- Share your feelings regarding your testing and results (disappointment, excitement, jealousy, envy, contentment, happiness, frustration, etc.).

- Describe what worked well for your team. Describe what didn't work well and what would have improved the situation.

To summarize the purpose for and methods of academic and emotional lesson integration, it may help to post "Steps to Achieving Academic and Emotional Intelligence" (Figure 2.1, repeated on page 18) as a visual reminder.

When beginning the integration process, remember that the first step is to create a classroom environment that feels open, honest, and caring. Students can have input in creating such an environment with the No Fear plan that should be made at the beginning of the school year. Next, in considering the definition of learning, remember to include not only acquired *knowledge* and understanding of *skills* but also *disposition* toward and *feelings* about those skills. Reflective opportunities and feedback regarding content and feelings take students beyond *surface knowledge*. Students discover new insights and make meaningful connections that allow the information to transfer to long-term memory and become *natural knowledge* (Caine & Caine, 1994).

FIGURE 2.1. Steps to Achieving Academic and Emotional Intelligence

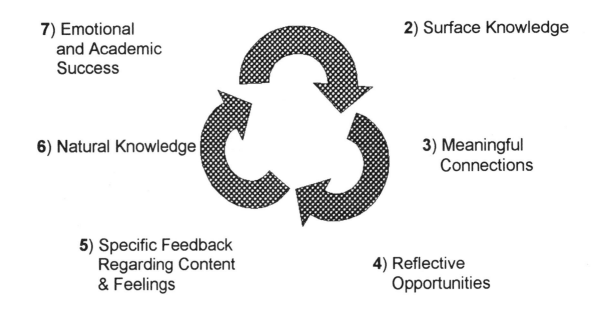

1) Positive Learning Climate

7) Emotional and Academic Success

2) Surface Knowledge

6) Natural Knowledge

3) Meaningful Connections

5) Specific Feedback Regarding Content & Feelings

4) Reflective Opportunities

3

Teaching Emotional Intelligence

Individuals who are "people-smart" have an advantage in life. Social skills, which come from emotional intelligence, are a key to success in a multitude of life situations:

- Sports activities

- Working with others on the job (communication skills for the workplace)

- Career readiness

- Successful friendships

- Healthy relationships

- Resolving anger without violence

Some people are born with a natural ability to "catch on" to social skills, enabling them to be socially successful early in life. They understand their own feelings and recognize these feelings in others. They can read signals their peers give and instantly know where they stand in these relationships. In short, these people are emotionally and socially in tune and aware.

Others must be taught these skills, which will increase their acceptance and proficiency when they interact in the "real world." We must not assume that all students become more socially and emotionally adept as they mature and gain academic skills. Instead, we teachers must foster their social and emotional attributes through their daily living to ensure that all students have the opportunity for a well-rounded and successful future.

Sports Activities

Most children begin participating in some type of sports activity at a very young age. There are certain unspoken rituals and practices involved in each game that must be learned for an individual to be successful. For instance, there is an enormous difference in the amount of acceptable referee involvement in baseball versus soccer. In a baseball game, it is common for players, coaches, and spectators to argue with umpires when they disagree with them. In soccer, this sort of harassment of referees is not tolerated.

Some children have a natural disposition for the social skills involved in various sports events; some learn by observing peers and/or parents who attend the games. Some children don't ever seem to "get it." These children do not have a natural disposition for social skills. We can help these children become more socially adept during physical education classes, recess, or intramural sporting events.

Teenagers with undeveloped social and emotional skills rant and rave from the stands, scream obscenities at the referee or coach, and embarrass everyone within a 50-foot radius. We wonder how a person can be 13 years old and behave so badly in public and be totally unaware of how this behavior affects others. This person does not naturally possess awareness of self and others, insight, or a perceptive nature. This individual needs guidance in learning the social skills that most of us recognize as obvious and acceptable.

Because individuals are involved in sports, games, or interactive hobbies throughout their lives, teachers can help students develop their self-awareness, self-responsibility, and self-assertiveness, when appropriate. When we observe students lacking in these skills, we can take a few minutes to discuss with our classes acceptable and nonacceptable behavior related to sporting events and games. Students who are more socially savvy can express how it feels to sit next to a person at a football game who is ranting and raving at the referee. This description may help the less socially adept student gain some insight into the feelings and emotions of others.

Communication Skills for the Workplace

According to a 1995 study sponsored by the U.S. Department of Education, schools are not preparing students for the workplace—

and test scores, grades, and the school's reputation are not what impress future employers. The study says that when employers make hiring decisions, attitude, communication skills, and work experience are the criteria of most importance (Henry, 1995).

Statistics show that most of our students end up in careers in which they will have to make presentations on the job. These same future employees will be expected to interact successfully in teams to make decisions and solve problems. Students who are socially adept and work well with others will excel. For students who are not naturally people-smart, this becomes a huge problem. Take a look at the following example of two individuals at work who must communicate their ideas to the company.

Sally Sociability	*Less Able Leslie*
Makes eye contact with the audience	Looks at her shoes during presentation
Stands tall with confidence	Hunches her shoulders and folds her arms
Uses volume, pitch of voice, and rate of speech effectively	Speaks in a monotone
Watches the audience for body language	Is oblivious to audience signals
Uses effective verbal skills to get the message across	Does not have an organized or rehearsed presentation
Uses effective listening skills to assure audience of fairness	Does not listen to audience feedback
Welcomes questions at the end of her presentation	Is afraid to allow questions from the audience
Follows up her presentation with a letter of appreciation for attendance	Is so glad to be done that she doesn't think of it again

Now, although this example is a bit of an exaggeration, the point is that when we foster the emotional growth of our students, we aren't just fostering self-esteem. We are creating the possibility of a successful future for our students, whether the success is in the area of landing a big account for a company, promoting a wellness policy for fellow employees, or persuading a company to use a particular advertising campaign. Sally's presentation skills were effective because she has mastered many components of emotional intelligence, such as awareness of self and others and approval of self and others. These attributes allow her to look and feel confident during a presentation.

Just as presentation skills are important for job success, so are effective group interaction skills. In Howard Gardner's (1993) book

Multiple Intelligences, he talks about the "interpersonal intelligence." A person with high interpersonal intelligence is also emotionally intelligent. This individual knows how to facilitate, use voice expression to make a point, and use effective listening skills. Once again, some students have a natural tendency toward this intelligence while others have to be taught the basics of effective team interaction. Through cooperative learning, group problem-solving tasks, and classroom presentations, interpersonal skills can be practiced and refined for career readiness.

As teachers, we must give our students plenty of group interaction practice to enable them to refine these skills. It isn't enough to tell them to "get into groups and figure out this problem." We must actually teach them the social skills of acceptable and effective group interaction. Some teachers use a very structured approach, giving each student a role such as timekeeper, group leader, group recorder, and so on. By starting out with highly structured roles, each student learns to be a responsible member of the team. Another approach to teaching group interaction skills involves the assignment of sections or chunks of work to be accomplished in short time intervals. This approach can be seen in the following example:

- **Topic:**   The Love of Cleopatra and Mark Antony

  1. For 5 minutes, list as many adjectives as possible to describe the feelings between Cleopatra and Mark Antony.

  2. For the next 5 minutes, make a short timeline to show the sequential events of their love affair.

  3. For the last 5 minutes, decide as a team the main reasons for the suicides of Cleopatra and Mark Antony.

Student teams are more likely to stay focused and on task when their assignments are narrow in scope and require completion in a short time. This is an effective technique to teach teamwork skills.

Whether group interactions are highly structured or more relaxed and casual, specific social guidelines must be followed rigidly. As mentioned in Chapter 2, students and teachers should collaboratively design a No Fear plan with social rules that enable all students to feel emotionally safe and secure during group interactions. A No Fear plan may include such rules as "Students will show respect for self and others by listening politely when others are speaking."

Group interaction skills not only provide students with the social competence to become problem solvers and decision makers, but, more important, these skills teach our students to be more emotionally insightful and aware of human nature. This emotional insight develops through an increased ability to recognize and name feelings and emotions during a discussion, to understand the difference between feelings and actions, to perceive another's perspective, and to communicate assertively within specific guidelines.

Career Readiness Skills

Incorporating career readiness skills into the curriculum may not at first seem relevant for the enhancement of emotional intelligence. But in learning about their strengths and how they can productively use those strengths in the world of work, students gain confidence, self-worth, and pride. When students can derive true meaning from and develop an emotional attachment to a piece of information that is relevant in their own lives, they gain more than content knowledge. They achieve self-approval, approval from peers, an understanding of their individualism, and guidance in career decisions.

Specifically, how can career readiness programs increase emotional intelligence? Lynn Olson (1997), author of *The School-to-Work Revolution*, made visits across the country to see the benefits of these programs. Her findings included the following points:

- Career readiness programs motivate students to learn. Many students reported that they were more interested and more challenged by career-related courses than by more traditional academic course work. High motivation leads to academic success, which in turn leads to the emotional well-being of the student.

- Students who work in teams to solve career-related problems, use hands-on activities, and plan and complete projects feel they are learning more information.

- A high percentage of students engaged in career readiness programs were pursuing postsecondary education because they understood the relationship between learning and a good job.

- School-to-work programs encourage students to make plans for a career, think about a direction according to their strengths, and feel more optimistic about their futures.

In short, teachers who incorporate career readiness activities and lessons into the curriculum provide students with opportunities for strengthening their emotional welfare and outlook on life and for finding an appropriate direction for their futures.

Career readiness activities may include the following components:

- Guest speakers from various career fields

- Field trips to job sites

- Internships (paid or unpaid work experiences for students to help demonstrate practical applications of academic learning)

- Job shadowing (a 1- or 2-day visit to a work site to observe a specific career field)

- Mentoring (pairing a student with an adult role model who can guide him or her with career advice or decision making)

Career-based activities promote the use of interpersonal skills and personal reflections regarding the future, and they establish a purpose for school academics, leadership skills, and information organization. Emotional intelligence can be strengthened and enhanced when incorporated into the curriculum as a method of preparing students for the appropriate behaviors, social skills, and expectations of the workplace.

Having Successful Friendships

Can socially inept children actually be trained to make successful friendships? According to several documented programs, they can. Students in the third and fourth grades who were the least liked and least popular were coached in learning how to make friends. They were given six training sessions and learned the objectives of being "friendly, fun, and nice." These children were coached to behave more as their more popular counterparts did with their friends. One year after the coaching began, all selected students had surfaced solidly in the middle of the popularity spectrum (Asher & Williams, 1987). This type of training or coaching appears to be effective in teaching students the appropriate social/interpersonal skills needed for friendship.

As students learn the mechanics of suitable social behaviors, they may begin by "acting" or regurgitating the right response. The hope is that eventually when they see the benefits of these appropriate responses, the responses will become habitual. The more important prospect is that through these new behaviors, students begin the journey toward emotional intelligence by developing new insight, self-awareness, and understanding of their peers.

Through curriculum integration, students can read stories that deal with friendships. They can discuss whether the characters were good friends and, as a team, make a list of the characteristics of friendship. They can role-play situations to show appropriate and inappropriate friendships and discuss or write about a friend who did not show good friendship. Consider using the dialogue in Exhibit 3.1 for student discussion.

After reading a dialogue such as this one, students can engage in a wealth of stimulating activities to foster emotional growth. Some suggestions include the following activities:

- Have a classroom discussion about how and why this conversation deteriorated.

- Discuss the question, if these two characters had been adults, what conversation might have caused this same kind of heated argument?

- Students can rewrite the dialogue so the conversation doesn't escalate into a heated discussion.

- Role-play this dialogue, first as it is written and then a second time after students rewrite it to show a more appropriate conversation.

- In cooperative teams, students can decide which character was more at fault in the argument. Share why this character was more to blame than the other and what could be done the next time to avoid this situation.

- Students can write journal entries about the character they most identify with and why.

As you can see, there are many possible activities based on the sample dialogue. You may want to start your friendship training with an isolated excerpt such as the one provided, but eventually the excerpts should be taken from class content. For example, if during a Revolutionary War unit the class had just finished reading Nathan Hale's famous quote, "I regret that I have but one life to give for my country," students may be asked to write a dialogue between Nathan Hale and his fictitious best friend. The act of incorporating emotional intelligence training into the regular curriculum allows students to gain a deeper understanding about Nathan Hale and his ordeal and, at the same time, gives students the chance to reflect on friendship.

Having Healthy Relationships

Few of us, as educators, ever see the effects we may have on our students in terms of their lifelong relationships. We do have the power, however, to develop and foster the basis for their future relationships.

Thomas: Hey, Joe, how'd you like the Nintendo game I loaned you last night?

Joe: That explosion when the two planets collided was awesome!

Thomas: Yeah, that's my favorite part too. And then there's the black hole! When the alien gets whisked away into the black hole, it looks cool.

Joe: Oh, I never got to that part.

Thomas: Yeah, it's cool. So, where's my game? You brought it back, right?

Joe: Well, no, it's still at my house.

Thomas: What? You promised me that if I let you borrow it, you'd bring it to school today!

Joe: So, what's the big deal? I'll bring it tomorrow. Besides, it'll give me a chance to see the alien go into the black hole.

Thomas: That really ticks me off, man. You said you'd bring it back today. You're such a liar. I should have known I couldn't count on you. What a liar!

Joe: I ought to deck you for calling me a liar. I can't believe what a big deal you are making out of nothing. I'll bring your stupid game tomorrow. Geez, what a big baby!

Thomas: You'd better bring it tomorrow or you'll be real sorry.

Part of that training takes place when we discuss and include friendship activities in our lessons. But relationships, such as those between mother and son or husband and wife, are often much more complicated, strenuous, and unpredictable than friendships.

In cultivating positive and healthy relationships, we must first ask students to assess their own character strengths and weaknesses. As a personally meaningful activity that is not to be shared with the class, students can fill out the Relationship Self-Assessment provided in Table 3.1 to determine areas of character strengths and weaknesses. This assessment should be kept confidential; the students might write about it in their journals or reflect on it without input from other students.

Next, students fill out a Relationship Attribute sheet (Table 3.2) to show their priorities in seeking relationships with others. This should be compared with their own personal assessment scores in an attempt to give students some insights into their own relationship

TABLE 3.1 Relationship Self-Assessment

Rate your strengths and weaknesses, with 1 meaning that you totally disagree and 5 meaning that you totally agree.

1. I am usually very trusting of other people.	1	2	3	4	5
2. I am a very caring person when it comes to my family and friends.	1	2	3	4	5
3. I can easily tell when I have hurt someone's feelings by their body language.	1	2	3	4	5
4. When I know I have made someone feel bad, I try to talk to them.	1	2	3	4	5
5. When I argue with someone, I try to have self-control and not get angry.	1	2	3	4	5
6. My friends think of me as a good listener when they need to talk.	1	2	3	4	5
7. I feel it is important to talk about feelings and emotions.	1	2	3	4	5
8. When I'm an adult, I hope to have a long-term committed relationship.	1	2	3	4	5
9. Honesty is something that I value very much.	1	2	3	4	5
10. Most of my friends and family members feel that I can be counted on.	1	2	3	4	5

TABLE 3.2 Relationship Attributes

Now think about the attributes in others that are important to you in a relationship, whether it is with a parent, friend, or future spouse.

I hope to find a relationship with someone who . . .

1. Is usually very trusting of other people.	1	2	3	4	5
2. Is a very caring person when it comes to family and friends.	1	2	3	4	5
3. Can easily tell when he or she has hurt someone's feelings.	1	2	3	4	5
4. Talks to someone when he or she has made that person feel bad.	1	2	3	4	5
5. Tries to have self-control when he or she argues with someone.	1	2	3	4	5
6. Is a good listener when I need to talk.	1	2	3	4	5
7. Feels it is important to talk about feelings and emotions.	1	2	3	4	5
8. As an adult, hopes to have a long-term committed relationship.	1	2	3	4	5
9. Values honesty very much.	1	2	3	4	5
10. Can be counted on by friends and family members.	1	2	3	4	5

shortcomings in comparison to the attributes they desire in others for a healthy relationship. Students in Grades 4 through 8 can fill out the assessment and attribute sheet themselves; teachers of younger students may want to read and discuss each item with their classes.

Resolving Anger Without Violence

In reading the story of Thomas's first day of kindergarten in Exhibit 3.2, you can probably predict his future in a traditional school setting. Thomas is full of energy and enthusiasm, and he also has many aggressive tendencies. As his school years go on, he will become less and less popular with both his teachers and his fellow students. His aggressive nature does not fit in the typical classroom setting, and he does not have a natural disposition toward social skills. Because he will become more and more frustrated and less and less accepted, his aggression will naturally gain momentum. By the time

⋀ EXHIBIT 3.2. Thomas's First Day at School

Thomas couldn't wait for the first day of kindergarten. He had awakened at 5:00 A.M. for the past week and a half in anticipation of his big day. At last, Monday morning arrived. Thomas's mother drove him to school, walked him to his classroom, and introduced him to his new teacher, Ms. James. Thomas was so full of excitement and energy that he forgot himself and began running around the classroom. Ms. James put on her "disapproving face" and told Thomas that in *her* classroom students didn't run around like wild banshees. Later in the morning, Thomas was so thrilled to be meeting so many new classmates, he decided he needed to give them all a big hug. He got a little carried away and began picking the children up and swinging them around. Ms. James didn't like this behavior one bit and she told Thomas he would have to stand against the wall at recess time. At lunchtime, Thomas discovered he could entertain his new friends by making milk come out of his nose. The children all seemed pleased with his amusing talent, but Ms. James was not impressed. During story time, Thomas discovered that if he bent a paper clip just right, he could then push down on it and make it jump. This was great enjoyment for Thomas because it startled the girls. One girl got mad and told Ms. James that Thomas was "a pain." Then a lot of the other girls began turning on him and complaining. By the end of the day, Thomas felt frustrated and mad. He had tried so hard to make Ms. James and the other students like him. What was wrong with all of them? Why couldn't they see that he wanted to be their friend? Well, fine then. If they didn't want to be his friends, he didn't want to be their friend, either. When the children were dismissed, Thomas saw the tattletale girl bent over the drinking fountain. On an impulse, he ran over to her and pushed her head down hard so that she got all wet. Ms. James saw the incident, grabbed Thomas by the collar, and marched him to the parking lot where his mother was waiting for him. Thomas had completed his first day of kindergarten.

Thomas is in Grade 5 or 6, he will probably be known as a bully, and his aggression will be in full swing. As Thomas matures and finds himself in other social situations, such as sports, relationships, and jobs, he undoubtedly will carry his unacceptable and under-developed social aptitude with him.

Many children enter kindergarten or first grade without an understanding of social expectations. Some of these children begin their schooling with aggressive tendencies but learn about acceptable behavior through observation and peer interaction. However, other students never quite seem to get it, and these are the children we are failing. These are the students who need emotional intelligence training. These children need activities to teach them to be sensitive to the needs of others, to read the feelings of their peers, the techniques of effective oral interaction, and the mechanics of proper behavior in various social settings. These same students need to be coached to give appropriate responses when they are feeling hurt. Thomas's pushing the little girl's head in the drinking fountain might have been a teachable moment. Ms. James might have taken some time to talk to Thomas about his reasons for his actions and discussed alternatives to the aggressive action he chose.

Research shows that children who enter first grade with disruptive and aggressive tendencies often become delinquents by the time they are teenagers. Later in life, these same students are more likely to commit serious, violent crimes (Huesmann, Eron, & Warnicke-Yarmel, 1987). Fortunately, research also shows that violence prevention programs can have a very positive effect in changing the attitudes and actions of these hostile students.

Rather than believe that disruptive and belligerent students are doomed to a life of crime we cannot prevent, we must instead strategically plan to teach correct and accepted behavioral responses. Most teachers don't have the time or training to add a separate program to the already full curriculum, but we can effectively integrate some type of "appropriate emotional response" training into our regular lessons.

As you begin to incorporate aggression or violence prevention techniques into your lessons, keep in mind that all students can benefit from learning appropriate social behaviors, and that by reflecting on actions and behaviors, students also gain a deeper understanding of the lesson content. The following list contains suggestions for violence prevention lessons:

- Cooperative teams can solve real-life problems.

- Read stories with conflict. Students can offer recommendations for solving the problems nonviolently.

- Students can write responses in journals regarding a personal conflict, a classroom conflict, or a content-related conflict.

- Students can be asked to put themselves in the place of a character or another student. This enables thoughtful reflection.

- Students can cut out articles on violent crime from the newspaper, and the class can decide how the problem could have been resolved in a nonviolent way.

- Students can use the following problem-solving techniques in their activities:

  1. State the problem.

  2. Brainstorm solutions.

  3. Narrow the number of solutions to a small number of workable ones.

  4. Select the final best solution.

- Students can role-play scenes showing appropriate and inappropriate methods of solving anger issues.

- Show a video of a violent confrontation and discuss with the class the steps that led to the violence and how it could have been prevented.

- Have students make a list of five events that would make them really angry and five nonviolent ways to deal with those events.

- Play "What's my emotion?"

  1. Students state, "I believe that I should go home now."

  2. They must say this statement to show the following feelings:

     a. They really don't want to go home.

     b. They are really excited about going home.

     c. They want to go home but the person they are talking to does not.

     d. They don't want to go home but the person they are talking to does.

  3. Students try to guess the emotion being portrayed.

Summarizing Lifelong Benefits

Remember that social skills come from emotional intelligence, and some of our students are not born with a natural disposition toward these skills. In addition, when students don't have positive role models in the home, they do not see the appropriate methods of dealing with anger, hurt, or frustration. Educators can incorporate simple techniques into their daily lessons that give students opportunities to achieve perceptiveness about and awareness of their own behaviors and those of others. These techniques, when practiced and implemented, will benefit students in their personal and professional lives. Specific response areas to explore with students include the following:

- Sports activities

- Career readiness skills

- Healthy relationships

- Communication skills for the workplace

- Successful friendships

- Resolving anger without violence

PART II

Components of Emotional Intelligence

4

Awareness of Self and Others

He dejectedly walks into his eighth-grade classroom, throws his backpack on the floor, and slides into his seat. He wears a wrinkled T-shirt with dirty jeans. No time was taken to comb his hair or wash his face. The classic body language is easy to decipher—poor posture, arms folded, head down, and no eye contact. His teachers aren't sure if he is incapable or incorrigible, but because he is not a distraction, he mostly goes unnoticed. During the course of the math period, he is not forced to interact with any of his classmates, so he allows himself to become lost in a daydream. The plots of his daydreams vary from day to day, but the underlying theme is the same. He is in control of his life. People rely on him to save them or protect them, and he is always successful in conquering the "bad guys." After rescuing a family from a burning building, destroying an enemy aircraft, or saving an entire town from an approaching flood, he comes to the final chapter of the daydream. He is praised and rewarded for his tireless efforts, masterful skills, and brave actions. He is respected, looked up to, and important in the eyes of the community.

The period bell rings. He snaps out of the daydream, slowly puts his work materials into his backpack, saunters out of the math classroom and continues on to his next class.

This student is in an emotional crisis. He feels no control over the events in his life; his body language and appearance indicate his low self-worth, and he appears to have no friends.

To more clearly explain the scene described above, we need to first define the term *self-awareness*, which is an integral component

FIGURE 4.1. Components of Emotional Intelligence

- **Awareness of Self and Others**

- Approval of Self and Others

- Mastering Self-Responsibility

- Finding Personal Meaning

- Valuing Honesty and Ethics

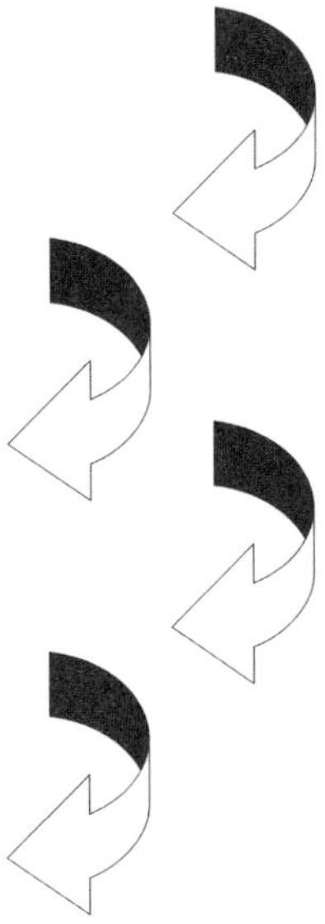

of emotional intelligence. However, even though self-awareness is only one part of emotional intelligence, it is a link in the chain of characteristics that all work together to define true emotional intelligence.

To gain understanding of self-awareness, consider the attributes of self-concept combined with knowledge of oneself. *Self-concept* refers to the totality of a complex, organized, and dynamic system of learned beliefs, attitudes, and opinions that each person holds to be true about his or her personal existence (Purkey, 1988). These beliefs, when combined with a cognizant awareness, or true understanding, of one's strengths, limitations, abilities, and disabilities, form self-awareness (see Figure 4.1).

Cognitive Consciousness

Every day, as our students set foot into the classroom, they must choose the level of consciousness with which to function. Students who have some self-awareness abilities may truly make a conscious decision to function at a certain level for that day. For instance, Tina may walk through the classroom doors thinking to herself, "Linda and I sure had trouble getting along yesterday. I'm going to really work at being patient with her today." Albert may come to school thinking, "I totally bombed that math test yesterday. I'm going to take notes today and pay attention so I'll score higher on the next test."

A student existing without cognitive consciousness or conscious decisions and thought processes is perpetuating low self-esteem. This student is also not very likely to be cognizant or aware of the emotions and feelings of his or her fellow students. Lack of awareness of self and others can cause major social problems as well as lifelong dilemmas. We can't expect our students to be empathetic about fellow classmates when they have no inkling of their own feelings and emotions.

The ability to feel empathy for the plight of another individual can come only through insightful self-awareness. How can children understand the hurt look on another child's face when they have never recognized the signs of hurt in themselves?

The impact of teaching self-awareness, which leads to an understanding of others, is acute in today's world. The capacity to feel empathy for others is an attribute that comes into play throughout our lifetimes. We need empathy to maintain an enduring relationship. We must understand and use empathy in our careers, with our families, and in our parenting. A lack of compassion for others can lead to the violent acts that we are suffering in our schools today. The complete lack of social conscience, seen in child molesters, psychopaths, and assassins, shows the emotional detachment of individuals who never gained self-awareness and therefore never gained empathy for others.

The teacher can foster a more conscious awareness within students in several ways:

▶ Create a classroom environment where open thought and exploration are safe. If students know that they can express opinions without repercussions, they are more likely to participate in the discussion.

▶ Learning by exploring motivates students to search for answers rather than passively memorize information. For example, if the lesson's objective is for the students to learn about vertebrates and invertebrates, the teacher may open the unit by saying, "Choose your favorite animal with a backbone and your favorite animal without a backbone. Compare and contrast other characteristics of these two animals." This open-ended lesson is more likely to lead students to search for information because they are permitted to explore and choose topics of interest to them.

▶ Specific class discussion formats sometimes lead students to extract greater meaning from the conversation and become thoroughly involved. In addition, they have an opportunity to "read" the emotions of their fellow students. Here is one idea for this type of discussion:

- Students form discussion groups of four to five.

- The teacher assigns a relevant topic (or a student-generated one).

- Each student gets four cards that say the following:
    1. My feeling is . . .
    2. I agree with you because . . .
    3. I disagree with you because . . .
    4. I'd also like to add that . . .

- When each group member has used at least three of the four cards, he or she may elect to end the discussion until a new topic has been generated.

Metacognition

True self-awareness involves a high level of intellect. For our students to achieve true self-awareness, they must use metacognitive skills. This involves becoming aware of one's own thought processes. In other words, *students learn to think about their thinking!* Self-awareness mastery is accomplished when a student recognizes what he or she is feeling and *why* he or she is feeling it. A student's self-awareness inner dialogue after a teacher returns an assignment to a student with a relatively low grade on it might be similar to Exhibit 4.1.

In a perfect world, the student dialogue in Exhibit 4.1 would be the norm for reflective thinking. But in reality, students must be *taught* how to proceed through this metacognitive thought process. We must give them the tools for determining their feelings and understanding how they feel about those feelings. We should begin teaching students to use a metacognitive thought process as soon as they start school.

We begin developing self-awareness with our very earliest experiences. We continue to develop and maintain self-awareness throughout the span of our lives through the process of having an experience, reflecting on that experience, and absorbing what others tell us about our experience. We also reflect on our actions with regard to the experience and compare them with our expectations and the expectations of others. We then compare our characteristics and accomplishments with those of others, and in doing this, we form extensions of our self-awareness.

Ms. Crosby makes me so mad. Who does she think she is to put down my work?

OK, maybe I didn't put in enough effort last night, but does that give her the right to cut down my writing?

So, what am I really feeling here? Is it anger? No, what I'm really feeling is hurt. My feelings are hurt because Ms. Crosby didn't have a positive reaction to my work.

Are my feelings valid? Well, I guess I have the right to feel hurt, because I like Ms. Crosby's approval. But on the other hand, I have to admit that I didn't work as hard on the assignment as I usually do.

So I understand my feelings of hurt, but I'm going to choose to take her criticism constructively and spend more time on my next assignment.

Three important aspects of self-awareness that affect overall well-being in life are physical self-awareness, academic self-awareness, and social self-awareness.

Physical Self-Awareness

Physical self-awareness involves all that is tangible, such as what one looks like; the clothes, hairstyle, jewelry, and so on that one wears; and what kind of home one lives in.

Academic Self-Awareness

Academic self-awareness is related to understanding how well one does in school with regard to achievement, grades, and concept understanding. When children have very little academic success, academic self-concept naturally suffers. However, when these low achievers are fully aware of scholastic weaknesses and are functioning in a cognitively conscious state, they are more open to strategies to increase academic performance.

When students are low achievers in many areas but have definite strengths in one or two particular areas, such as math, reading, art, or music, they have opportunities for high academic self-awareness *if this strength is recognized and fostered.* Once again, the key to success is the student's cognizant awareness of these strengths. On the other hand, when students are academically successful in many areas, the chances of high academic self-awareness are very favorable, especially when students have had opportunities to reflect on specific successes, why they occurred, and how they feel about those successes.

Social Self-Awareness

Social self-awareness refers to how one relates to other people, whether they are peers, coworkers, family members, or strangers. Students need occasions during which they can think insightfully about their positive and negative interactions with peers. It is vital that they learn the techniques of "reading" the emotional reactions of their peers.

Daniel Goleman (1997) cites tests with more than 7,000 people in the United States and 18 other countries. The results show how people benefit from the ability to read feelings from nonverbal body language cues, including better emotional adjustment, greater popularity, and a more outgoing and sensitive personality.

In relating social self-awareness to the lethargic eighth-grade student who moves in slow motion, does not interact with peers, and finds solace in daydreams, let's now consider the condition of his self-awareness. With regard to his physical self-awareness, we can see from the little effort he puts into his appearance, he is greatly lacking in pride and confidence. His appearance alone should be a warning sign to teachers that his emotional well-being is suffering. He has not learned to ask himself why he doesn't take pride in his appearance and how he feels about his lack of pride. Somewhere along the line, he has chosen to function at a low level of consciousness with regard to his appearance.

Academically, his teachers aren't certain if his insufficient effort is truly a lack of ability or an act of belligerence. Because this boy is primarily walking around in a fog, his chances of building social self-awareness are very poor. For as long as he continues down this path with no training whatsoever in understanding his own feelings, the feelings of others, or appropriate methods to deal with these feelings, his feelings of self-worth will continue to decrease. He will compare his actions with the actions from his daydreams and classify himself as a failure. He will watch his classmates gain higher self-awareness as a result of their accomplishments (and self-reflections about those accomplishments), but will he be trained to question himself as to why he is not achieving these same kinds of accomplishments? In short, without intervention so this child can realize some positive feedback and self-awareness, he will continue to spiral down the isolated and lonely tunnel toward an unfulfilled life.

Honesty with oneself and a cognizant effort to perceive feelings in others is the key to self-awareness. It is the courage to look at what we fear, what we believe, what we like about ourselves, and what we find distasteful in ourselves. Self-awareness also involves taking the initiative to be insightful in regard to others and to recognize when someone is feeling hurt, angry, joyous, or sad. Finally, self-awareness means taking perceived information and making decisions such as how one feels, why one feels that way, and what should be done about it.

On the following pages are several content-related self-awareness activities. They are categorized by appropriate grade levels.

Self-Awareness Activity 1

INTRODUCING MYSELF TO ME

Level: K through 4

Subject areas: Science, Language Arts

Directions:

The class takes a nature walk. This could take place on the school grounds, in a nearby park, or in a neighborhood. Students are asked to find a beautiful object from nature, such as a rock, leaf, or twig. When students go back to the classroom, they decide how this object from nature is similar to them and how it is different from them. The middle column of the reporting sheet should show similarities between the student and the natural object.

Kindergarten through grade one students may illustrate their comparisons, rather than list them.

ME	ME and NATURE	NATURE OBJECT
Size:	Size:	Size:
Shape:	Shape:	Shape:
Outside Covering:	Outside Covering:	Outside Covering:
Colors:	Colors:	Colors:
Feeling:	Feeling:	Feeling:
Needs:	Needs:	Needs:

Self-Awareness Activity 1

INTRODUCING MYSELF TO ME

Level: K through 4

Subject area: Science, Language Arts

Directions:

After filling out the comparison chart, students can create a Venn diagram to show ways they are similar to and different from their natural objects.

Kindergarten through grade one students should do this exercise with teachers modeling.

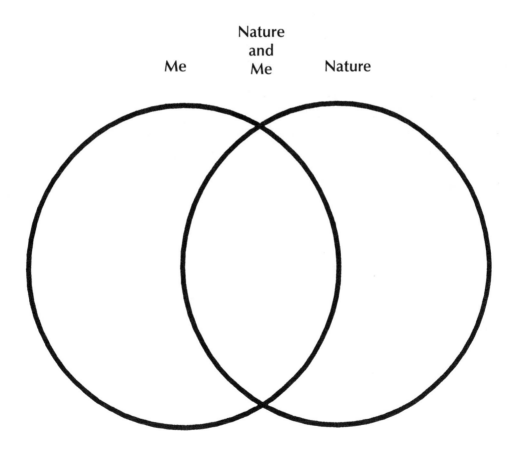

Me   Nature and Me   Nature

Self-Awareness Activity 1

INTRODUCING MYSELF TO ME

Level: 5 through 8

Subject areas: Science, Social Studies, Language Arts

Directions:

Students research various famous people in a curriculum-related area. They may investigate famous scientists who made important discoveries or heroes or heroines from history. Each student is to choose one person he or she greatly admires. After choices have been made, students compare and contrast themselves with this person and fill out the following comparison chart.

ME	BOTH OF US	Name: _____
Appearance:	Appearance:	Appearance:
Abilities:	Abilities:	Abilities:
Interests:	Interests:	Interests:
Intelligence Strengths:	Intelligence Strengths:	Intelligence Strengths:
Work Ethic:	Work Ethic:	Work Ethic:
Emotional Strengths:	Emotional Strengths:	Emotional Strengths:

Self-Awareness Activity 1

INTRODUCING MYSELF TO ME

Level: 5 through 8

Subject areas: Science, Language Arts

Directions:
After filling out the comparison chart, students can create a Venn diagram to show ways they are similar to and different from their chosen hero or heroine.

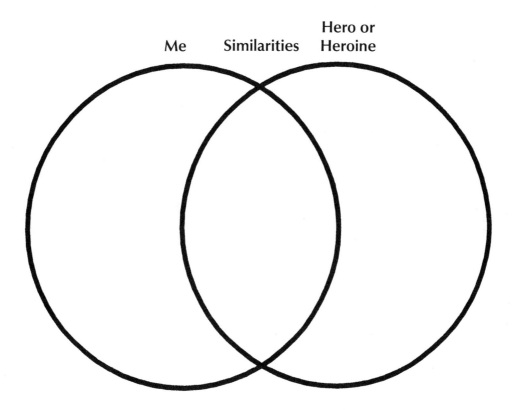

Self-Awareness Activity 2

MY FOUR FEELINGS

Level: 2 through 8

Subject areas: All

Directions:

Copy the following four sentence beginnings on each of four cards and duplicate the cards so each student receives a set. Students form teams of four to five members. The teacher assigns content-related topics for discussion. Some suggested topics are provided in Self-Awareness Activity 2 (page 47). Each student receives the four cards, which allows him or her to speak in the discussion. When all students have used their four cards, they end the discussion until a new topic has been generated.

MY FEELING IS . . .	**I AGREE WITH YOU BECAUSE . . .**
I DISAGREE WITH YOU BECAUSE . . .	**I'D ALSO LIKE TO ADD THAT . . .**

Self-Awareness Activity 2

MY FOUR FEELINGS

Level: 2 through 4

Subject areas: All

Directions:
Below are Reading, Social Studies, and Science questions for which the self-awareness cards may be used.

Reading

- How did this character feel?
- What could he or she have done?
- How would you have felt if this had happened to you?
- What was the scariest part of the story?
- What was the funniest part of the story?

Social Studies

- What does "freedom" mean to you?
- What should the president do about poverty?
- What should schools do about violence?
- How do you feel about gun control?
- Tell what your state flag symbolizes.

Science

- What advice would you give people if a supernova was about to explode?
- What would be the benefits of being a snake?
- List three words that best describe the bottom of the ocean.
- What should we be doing to conserve water?
- What is your favorite insect and why?
- Which is more frightening, a volcano or an earthquake? Why?

Self-Awareness Activity 2

MY FOUR FEELINGS

Level: 5 through 8

Subject areas: All

Directions:
Use sentence starters, such as the Reading, Social Studies, and Science examples below, to foster the integration of content with personal feelings and emotions.

Reading

- The exact moment the story came to a dramatic climax was when . . .
- The character who truly demonstrated confidence and strength was . . .
- The part of the book that brought the most emotion to the surface was . . .
- The most appealing setting throughout the book was . . .
- The character who is least likely to have a successful life was . . .
- The character who is most likely to have a successful life was . . .

Social Studies

- I could most identify with the (Union/Confederate) side because . . .
- To avoid the Civil War, President Lincoln could have . . .
- The most honorable person during the Revolutionary War was . . .
- Patrick Henry was (brave/weak) because . . .
- The single most significant act George Washington did was . . .
- To have the biggest impact on reducing school violence, . . .

Science

- Water conservation should begin with . . .
- If only one disease could be funded for research, that disease should be . . .
- My concern about cloning is . . .
- The most interesting function of the brain is . . .
- The natural disaster I'm most afraid of is . . . because . . .

Self-Awareness Activity 3

"READING" BODY LANGUAGE

Level: K through 8

Subject areas: Social Studies, Language Arts, Science

Directions:

Teach students to read about the four types of body language (see below). Next, find pictures relating to the current content of your studies. Ask students (grade 3 through 8) to study the body language of people in the pictures and make inferences about the feelings and intentions of those people. Last, you may want students to write a reflection paragraph about their insights.

Kindergarten through 2nd-grade students may share their reflectons orally or by drawing pictures. Visuals illustrating the four types of body language would aid understanding.

Four Types of Body Language

- Gestures—An open attitude includes palms up, open hands, and arms outstretched. Defensive or bored signs include arms and legs crossed, head low on chest, hands rubbing eyes, and wringing hands.

- Facial expressions—Favorable reactions include ends of the mouth turned up and direct eye contact. Ends of the mouth turned down or straight lips can indicate boredom or disagreement. Furrowed foreheads or eyebrows show that the listener does not approve or believe what is being said.

- Posture—When a person sits in a slumped position and is leaning away from the speaker, it often shows a feeling of being trapped, bored, or restless. When a person leans forward with straight posture, it is more likely they are interested in what the speaker has to say.

- Movement—When a person walks with a purpose, has straight posture, and is making eye contact, he or she is showing confidence and competence.

Self-Awareness Activity 4

FEELING CLUES

Level: K through 8

Subject areas: Language Arts /Social Studies

Directions:

Students read a story, article, or excerpt. Based on the verbal language, author's description, and character's actions, students look for clues about the character's feelings. As students read and discuss, they refer to a list of "feeling" words for assistance. They may circle words they feel describe the character's emotional state.

Kindergarten and 1st-grade teachers may want to use pictures to demonstrate the feelings to be discussed.

Feeling Words

Accepting	Lonely	Tender
Unworthy	Lighthearted	Relaxed
Spiteful	Lovable	Reserved
Untrusting	Loving	Assertive
Revengeful	Bold	Forgiving
Sensible	Broad-minded	Calm
Friendly	Weak	Funny
Careful	Caring	Gentle
Nurturing	Stable	Strong
Happy	Thankful	Compassionate
Frustrated	Patient	Peaceful
Tolerant	Considerate	Understanding
Angry	Hurt	Depressed

Self-Awareness Activity 5

AWARENESS ALERT!

Level: K through 4

Subject areas: Language Arts, Social Studies, Science

Directions:

Students are introduced to a self-rating scale that they use to show their feelings about various curriculum-related readings, discussions, or events. They are to indicate their feelings by circling the point at which they agree. By using this scale, students can begin to identify and understand their own ideals, beliefs, and viewpoints, and therefore gain more self-awarenes.

Kindergarten and 1st-grade teachers may prefer a sad and happy face scale on which students circle their feelings based on the teacher's oral questions.

Self-Rating Scale

Super good stuff --------------------------------------- Bad news

Easy! --- What???

Feels happy! -- Feels sad

I can use this --- I'll never use this

I agree -- I don't agree

Free feeling --- Tight feeling

Fun --- Boring

I liked it--- I didn't like it

Self-Awareness Activity 5

AWARENESS ALERT!

Level: 2 through 4

Subject areas: Language Arts, Social Studies, Science

Directions:

The following story could be read to students. Before a class discussion on the story, students do independent self-reflection by filling out the Self-Rating Scale on page 52.

Rosie sat at her desk working on the math test. "Boy," she thought, "this test is sure harder than I thought it was going to be. I don't understand how to do some of these problems."

Just then, Rosie glanced over to the girl who sat across from her. Her name was Ruth Anne, and she hadn't been very nice to Rosie all year. Ruth Ann was stretching her neck and looking on the desk of the boy who sat in front of her. "She's cheating!" thought Rosie. "She's copying down the answers to the math test questions! I'll bet she didn't even study last night."

Rosie felt angry that Ruth Ann was cheating and might even get a good grade without doing any studying. She had to decide what to do. If she told on Ruth Ann, some of the kids might call her a "tattle-tale." Ruth Ann would be even more mean and nasty to Rosie than she already was. She could decide to talk to Ruth Ann about it and let her know that she would have to tell the teacher if she ever did it again. Or she could just ignore the whole thing and finish her test.

Rosie decided she would talk to Ruth Ann at recess and let her know cheating was wrong and she would have to let the teacher know the next time it happened.

How do you feel about Rosie's decision? Would you have done anything differently?

Self-Awareness Activity 5

AWARENESS ALERT!

Level: 5 through 8

Subject areas: Language Arts, Social Studies, Science

Directions:

Students are introduced to a self-rating scale, on which they can show their feelings about various curriculum-related readings, discussions, or events. They are to indicate their feelings by circling the point at which they agree. By using this scale, students can begin to identify and understand their own ideals, beliefs, and viewpoints and therefore gain more self-awareness.

Self-Rating Scale

Complete agreement ------------------------- Total disagreement

Easy concept --------------------------------- Difficult concept

Pleasant feeling------------------------------- Bothersome feeling

Important ------------------------------------- Unnecessary

Inspiring--------------------------------------- Inhibiting

Loose feeling---------------------------------- Restrictive feeling

Creative --------------------------------------- Unimaginative

Useful information---------------------------- Not relevant

Exciting concept ----------------------------- Dull concept

Appropriate action--------------------------- Inappropriate action

Helpful information -------------------------- Useless information

High enjoyment------------------------------- No enjoyment

Self-Awareness Activity 5

AWARENESS ALERT!

Level: 5 through 8

Subject areas: Language Arts, Social Studies, Science

Directions:

Students read the following excerpt about Revolutionary War patriot Patrick Henry. Before a class discussion on the excerpt, students do independent self-reflection by filling out the Self-Rating Scale on page 54.

Patrick Henry, American Patriot

Patrick Henry was an American orator and statesman whose exuberant passion and patriotism was influential in leading the colonies toward revolution. Henry was a storekeeper and then a farmer. After failing at both of these professions, he became a prominent lawyer. By 1765, Henry was a member of the colonial legislature of Virginia, the House of Burgesses, where he introduced seven resolutions against the Stamp Act. Five of his resolutions were carried by a majority vote, and all seven of his resolutions were printed in the colonial newspaper.

When Patrick Henry was reelected to the House of Burgesses in 1769, he joined a radical group of dissidents who wanted to break away from England. The House of Burgesses was dissolved in 1774, and at that time, Henry became a member of the Revolutionary Convention of Virginia. In speaking before the convention on March 23, 1775, he pleaded with Virginians to take a state of defense. His famous speech is remembered for these words:

"It is in vain, Sir, to extenuate the matter. Gentlemen may cry peace, peace—but there is not peace. The war is actually begun! Why stand we here idle? What is it that gentlemen wish? What would they have? Is life so dear, or peace so sweet, as to be purchased at the price of chains and slavery?! Forbid it, Almighty God! I know not what course others may take; but as for me, give me liberty or give me death!"

Summary

By integrating self-awareness activities into content areas, we allow students to combine their past beliefs with a new awareness of their opinions, feelings, and viewpoints based on content materials. From self-awareness content activities, our students can learn to make conscious decisions about the academic levels they wish to achieve on a particular day.

Teachers can enhance the self-awareness process by establishing a safe, yet challenging environment for students in which all thoughts and ideas are valued. Inquiry learning, or learning by discovery and exploration, may be incorporated into daily activities. Open classroom discussions must be valued as a component of a successful lesson rather than as a time consuming extra step. And the use of metacognitive thinking (the ability to think about one's feelings regarding the presented information) must become a piece of the students' assessment.

Educators can have a direct impact on the well-being of their students by honoring and fostering the physical self-awareness, academic self-awareness, and social self-awareness of their students.

5

Approval of
Self and Others

If you doubt you can accomplish something, then you can't accomplish it. You have to have confidence in your ability, and then be tough enough to follow through.

—Rosalynn Carter

The focus of Chapter 4 was the importance of teaching students the skills of self-awareness. When we aren't aware of our physical, academic, and social selves with clarity, it is difficult to gain mastery of self-approval. Thus, self-approval is the second link in the chain of components of emotional intelligence (see Figure 5.1).

The way we interpret our actions, beliefs, feelings, and life situations affects our ability to accept or approve of ourselves. If children believe other students don't want to be their friends, they begin to withdraw socially, and therefore, they will have no friends. If students believe they can't succeed in math, they feel depressed or passive and won't give math their best efforts. Therefore, these students won't be successful in understanding math concepts. Students who believe they can't do anything without teacher assistance become inadequate and dependent because of those beliefs. When children

FIGURE 5.1. Components of Emotional Intelligence

- ■ Awareness of Self and Others

- ■ **Approval of Self and Others**

- ■ Mastering Self-Responsibility

- ■ Finding Personal Meaning

- ■ Valuing Honesty and Ethics

think they are stupid and incapable of achievement, they feel worthless, do not accept themselves, and perhaps even hate themselves.

Self-approval, our second link in the emotional intelligence chain, can be realized only if children are aware of both their strengths and weaknesses regarding their physical, academic, and social beings. Self-approval is the ability to understand and accept *"I feel what I feel, I believe what I believe, I like what I like, and I am capable of what I am capable of."* In other words, it is the willingness to hold onto and celebrate our ethics, our values, our prejudices, our blemishes, our strengths, and our weaknesses. By the same token, our students must learn that their classmates are entitled to be who they are, with their own sets of beliefs and values as well. They must become adept at seeing another's point of view and finding empathy for others, and this can happen only when children have first discovered how to value themselves.

Self-approval involves making an agreement with oneself to accept, love, appreciate, and support oneself, imperfections and all, at this very minute. It involves the acknowledgment of others with different beliefs, attitudes, and values and being open to those differences. A child who learns empathy is a child who can "walk in another's moccasins" and feel what that individual is feeling.

Learning empathy, which is a characteristic of one who has mastered self-approval, has academic value as well as lifelong benefits. In a test involving 1,011 children, those who showed an ability to read the nonverbal feeling cues of others performed better in school even though their IQs were no higher than students who were less skilled in reading nonverbal feeling messages (Nowicki & Duke, 1989).

In addition to empathy, whether students are inherently pessimists or optimists has a great deal to do with how well they master the art of self-approval. Consider an example of two students who both studied for a difficult science test. Student 1 received a grade of D and Student 2 received a grade of C–. Student 1 saw this grade as a learning experience, and the reaction to this grade was hopeful, active, and positive. The student chose to improve future test scores through planning, getting advice, and finding new study techniques. Student 2 was dismally disappointed with the grade of C–. This student assumed there was absolutely nothing that could be done to improve the situation. This student thinks the teacher obviously gave a poor test, or "I am just doomed to be a failure."

The above example demonstrates how optimism can be a good predictor of student academic success. When students use self-awareness in relation to their academic problems and then find self-approval for the efforts they put forth, they are using optimistic strategies that lead to future success.

According to Daniel Goleman (1997), we may be born with a predisposition toward optimism or pessimism, but our negative or positive outlook can be learned. When students meet challenges and succeed in some form, they strengthen the self-approval link. These students are more likely to take risks, search for new challenges, and develop more positive outlooks on life. As educators, we can lead our students through activities that give them the opportunities for self-awareness followed by strategies for developing self-approval. What follows is a simulated problem that calls for the art of self-approval. Follow the steps taken and use the Steps to Self-Approval charts with students as needed.

(text continues on page 61)

Steps to Self-Approval

Directions:

Take students through the steps in the left-hand column to resolve conflict and find self-approval (appropriate for Grades 3 through 8).

Describe a physical or social event that was uncomfortable for or upsetting to you.	*Example:* Jack harasses me at school every day by taking my stuff, yanking my hair, and grabbing me. Yesterday, because I wouldn't pay attention to him, he threw my homework into a mud puddle. That was the last straw!
Regarding this event, make a list of the following items: • The thoughts that went through your head • The images (mind pictures) you saw in your mind • Your self-talk during the event	*Example:* I was thinking about how I could get back at him. I wanted to push him or hit him hard and make him fall into the mud, so that he could see how it feels to be humiliated. I tried to tell myself to stay calm, but I didn't do a very good job of it.
Regarding this event, what reactions or responses did you show and do you *approve* of these responses at this time?	*Example:* I yelled at him and used some cuss words because I was so angry. I don't approve of the screaming fit that I threw in front of everyone.
List the responses or actions you want to take in the future should an event like this happen again.	*Example:* I need to use assertive language with Jack so I won't always be the victim. The next time he harasses me, I will make sure that an adult knows what I have been putting up with.

Steps to Self-Approval

Directions:

Take students through the steps in the left-hand column to resolve conflict and find self-approval (appropriate for Grades 3 through 8).

Describe a physical or social event that was uncomfortable for or upsetting to you.	
Regarding this event, make a list of the following items: • The thoughts that went through your head • The images (mind pictures) you saw in your mind • Your self-talk during the event	
Regarding this event, what reactions or responses did you show and do you approve of these responses are you at this time?	
List the responses or actions you want to take in the future should an event like this happen again.	

The emotional intelligence chain starts with self-awareness, followed by self-approval. When self-awareness has not been achieved, it is a much bigger challenge to foster self-approval because of the missing link. The following story demonstrates this challenge.

Self-Approval for Lyndsay

"I was just born weird," Lyndsay is fond of saying. And in some respects, she is right. Lyndsay certainly doesn't follow the cookie cutter mold for the typical sixth-grade girl. Lyndsay has no real friends to speak of, and she has never learned to become aware of her appearance or her social skills. She reminds some people of an English sheep dog because of her large size, bushy hair, and clumsy mannerisms.

Lyndsay still remembers that time in the first grade when she cried because she didn't understand the assignment. Her teacher admonished her for not paying attention, and the boys who sat next to her laughed and called her a "cry baby." She tried hard to never cry like that again.

In the third grade, when Lyndsay begged her mother for some new clothes for the school year, her mother told her that they simply didn't have enough money for such frivolities. Her father told her that she wasn't much of a "looker" anyway, so she didn't need to worry about having pretty clothes.

Lyndsay has no siblings to hang out with. Her parents believe in the old saying, "Children should be seen and not heard," only in Lyndsay's case, they don't want to see her much, either. She is often banished to her bedroom so "the adults can talk." She amuses herself by sketching on her art pad, singing to the radio, or reading teen magazines. Lyndsay's parents have difficult work schedules and can't take time off to go to school events or conferences.

She is in the sixth-grade choir this year, and the school had been practicing for the big Winter Festival show for weeks and weeks. The day of the performance, Ms. Jensen, the choir director, had a long talk with the students. She instructed everyone to wear white shirts and blue pants or skirts. She reminded them of the proper way to file into the auditorium and how to stand on the risers. She told them that even though the show started at 7:00 P.M., she wanted everyone there half an hour early to line up and get ready. Lyndsay remembers how excited she was that day. She loved to sing, and when she stood with the large group in the auditorium, she wasn't afraid to belt it out for all to hear.

Mom and Dad were too busy to come to the show, but Ms. Jensen said that she would take Lyndsay. Although Lyndsay couldn't find a white shirt or a blue skirt, she felt that she had managed quite nicely. She had taken one of her dad's T-shirts for the top, and put it over an old blue dress that she had outgrown two years ago. The dress was too short and was very tight, but Lyndsay didn't care. She was going to sing her lungs out tonight.

When Lyndsay stepped out of the car with Ms. Jensen at her side, she began to hear the familiar snickers and chortling. "What kind of a get-up is that supposed to be?" and "I get it. Your old man wouldn't come so you took his shirt?" cried one of her fellow students.

Just as familiar as the laughter that she endured daily was Lyndsay's response. She turned around and began to wildly kick and smack whoever happened to be in her line of fire. She had become so used to this routine that it was second nature to her by now. Unfortunately, the smart-aleck boy who had started this scene didn't move in time to miss Lyndsay's left hook. Down he went with a thud, but he rose just as quickly. He was embarrassed and mad and he flew into Lyndsay to protect his failing ego.

Ms. Jensen had been shouting at the children to stop, but in light of the fact that both students were as big as she was, she did not enter the fray. By the time a large parent stepped in to pull the two children apart, Lyndsay was a mess. Her hair was dripping with sweat and mud. Her dad's T-shirt was filthy and torn. Her throat hurt from screaming at the boy and she certainly didn't feel like singing joyous winter songs at this point.

Ms. Jensen studied Lyndsay carefully. What life events had led this child to be ridiculed daily and react with an outburst of anger? Why has no one stepped in to help Lyndsay believe in herself? She put her arm around Lyndsay's muddy shoulder and quietly said, "Come on. Let's go to the bathroom and clean you up."

Lyndsay's story is all too familiar to most of us in education. This child has never learned self-awareness because she has been isolated from normal social settings. She has no siblings to interact with, and her parents basically don't want to be bothered with her. Without physical or social self-awareness, Lyndsay doesn't know how to dress or act appropriately. She has very little chance of ever gaining self-approval because she has missed the first link in the emotional intelligence chain. Lyndsay needs to develop the following attributes to realize self-awareness and self-approval:

1. To become consciously aware of her physical, academic, and social self

2. To become aware of and accepting of her beliefs, values, and opinions

3. To become aware of her own nonverbal messages as well as the nonverbal messages of others

4. To realize some success to discover self-approval

5. To make an agreement with herself to love herself with all of her flaws, strengths, and weaknesses

6. To make conscious decisions to turn bad situations into positive learning experiences

7. To practice actions and responses that are appropriate

8. To gain the empathy and understanding of others

On the following pages are some suggested activities to use with students to help them gain self-approval and the approval of others.

Self-Approval Activity 1

QUIET BALL

Level: K through 8

Subject areas: Language Arts, Social Studies, Science

Directions:

Students of all ages love the quiet ball game. This can be used as a daily warm-up activity or with content areas. The rules are simple. The class sits in a circle, preferably on the floor. A relevant topic is brought up (perhaps a current social or academic issue in the classroom). Students are asked to share their personal feelings about the topic when the quiet ball is thrown to them. They may elect to pass if they feel too uncomfortable. Only the student holding the ball may speak. No other student may pass judgment on the opinions of that student. When the quiet ball game has ended, no conversation from the game may be mentioned until the next round of Quiet Ball.

Example:

Teacher: Tell me which content area you personally are feeling pleased with right now and why you are feeling this way.

Student response: I'm feeling good about math right now because I've been working on my homework every night, and now I understand the parts that were confusing me.

Self-Approval Activity 2

MORNING CONNECTIONS

As students arrive at school each morning, they are asked to sit on the floor of their classroom in a circle. The school day begins with a morning connection that teaches children a method for enhancing self-approval. The teacher says an incomplete sentence or phrase, which could be content related. The teacher then gives an example of how to finish the sentence. Then the next child inserts her or his own ending. As the incomplete sentence goes around the circle, a method for encouraging self-approval is established in the first part of the day. It also allows teachers to focus on students who seemed troubled. As students see that the opinions and values of their peers vary greatly, they begin to relax with their own feelings and gain self-approval. Older students, who are more easily embarrassed about sharing their feelings, may need to start with topics that are comfortable for them, such as music, concerts, or sports. Sample Morning Connection Phrases for Grades K through 4 and 5 through 8 students follow on page 67.

Self-Approval Activity 2

MORNING CONNECTIONS

Level: K through 4

Subject areas: Language Arts, Social Studies, Science

❖ **Famous/rich**

I would rather be _____ than _____ and it's OK to

feel that way because _____.

❖ **Beautiful/brilliant**

It's more important to be _____ than _____

because _____.

❖ **Creative/well-organized**

I would rather be _____ than _____

and my reasons are _____.

❖ **Good reader/good mathematician**

I prefer to be a _____ over being a _____

and I feel this way because _____.

❖ **Thousand dollars/thousand friends**

It's more important to have a _____ than a _____

because _____.

Self-Approval Activity 2

MORNING CONNECTIONS

Level: 5 through 8

Subject areas: Language Arts, Social Studies, Science

- One healthy outlet I can use when I am angry is . . .

- If I were to think intensely about my goals in life, I would feel . . .

- One area where I will concentrate and put forth energy today is . . .

- If I were to demonstrate empathy today, I would . . .

- An area of life where I am truly responsible is . . .

- I could become a better friend by . . .

- A healthy way to handle hurt feelings is . . .

- In thinking about my most difficult subject, I realize I could improve by . . .

- A healthy way for me to relax is to . . .

- An action that I took to avoid violence was . . .

- An academic area I am especially proud of is . . .

- If I were to take the time to learn a new activity, I would choose . . .

- If I were to watch someone's eyes and body language, I would see . . .

- If my best friend didn't see that I was hurt, I . . .

- When I think about my biggest fear, I feel _____ inside.

Self-Approval Activity 3

IF I WERE . . .

Level: K through 8

Subject areas: Language Arts, Social Studies, Science

Directions:

From current language arts, social studies, or science topics, students choose famous people and learn about the situations they experienced. Students then put themselves in the place of their chosen famous person, and decide on appropriate action. Next, students justify the reasons they approve of this action. Below are samples for Grades K through 4 and 5 through 8.

Grades K through 4 Model

Person	What happened	What would you do?	Why?
Goldilocks	Eating all of the porridge and breaking Baby Bear's chair.	Write a note to the bears telling them that I'll return with money to repay them.	This would be honest, and also the bears wouldn't be so mad at me.

Grades 5 through 8 Model

Person	Situation	Suggested Action	Justification
A colonist stamp agent	He sees angry colonists coming toward his store in a mob.	Lock the store and go out the back exit.	The colonists are too angry to deal with and there are so many of them that they won't listen to reason.

Self-Approval Activity 4

SELF-APPROVAL FOR THE FUTURE

Level: K through 4

Subject areas: Language Arts, Social Studies

Directions:
Brainstorm with children about the kinds of things they can perform proficiently and their preferences. It may be a physical activity, a friendship trait, an academic talent, and so on. Next, the students draw pictures showing a favorite thing they can do and a favorite thing they prefer.

Brainstorm List	*Things I Can Do Drawing*	*Things I Prefer Drawing*
Things I Can Do Brush my teeth Ride my bike Help my mom Read a lot of books **Things I Prefer** Hiking/backpacking PE instead of Math Basketball		

Self-Approval Activity 4

SELF-APPROVAL FOR THE FUTURE

Level: 5 through 8

Subject areas: Language Arts, Social Studies

Directions: Students put a check mark next to their abilities.

	Strong reading skills		Musically inclined
	Organized and good with details		Mechanically inclined
	Athletic ability		Good oral communication skills
	Creative writing skills		Good with animals
	Knowledge of gardening/plants		Able to speak foreign language
	Good with friendships		Strong mathematical skills
	Technical/computer skills		High physical endurance
	Able to play sports		Strong long-term memory

Students put a check mark next to their preferences regarding future careers.

	Working alone		Working in teams
	Nature vs. high tech		High tech vs. nature
	Working inside		Working outside
	Making my own decisions		Letting others make decisions
	Working with people		Working with animals
	Working with big equipment		Working with information
	Being extremely challenged		Taking it easy
	Dressing professionally		Dressing casually
	Active, noisy atmosphere		Quiet, low-key atmosphere
	Being fairly stationary		High physical activity

List any other abilities and/or preferences that you have here:

Self-Approval Activity 4

SELF-APPROVAL FOR THE FUTURE

Level: K through 8

Subject areas: Language Arts, Social Studies

Directions:

Students need opportunities to reflect on what they have discovered about themselves. They also need to be encouraged to explain why their abilities and preferences are valid as a way to promote self-approval.

Kindergarten through 2nd-grade students may illustrate or share discoveries orally.

Reflection Page
Write (or share orally) your discoveries regarding your abilities and preferences.

Self-Approval Activity 4

SELF-APPROVAL FOR THE FUTURE

Level: K through 4

Subject areas: Language Arts, Social Studies

Directions:

Students learn about various career pathways, which leads to enhanced self-approval. Using pictures, guest speakers, and classroom discussion, generate a list of careers and categorize these careers by whether they involve working with people, things, or information.

Career Pathways

Working with people	police officer, teacher, nurse, firefighter, psychologist, social worker, physical therapist, doctor, caseworker, salesperson

Working with things	forklift operator, architect, automotive technician, electrician, landscaper, farmer, computer technician, TV repair person

Working with information	accountant, business owner, administrative assistant, telephone operator, computer programmer, data entry worker

Self-Approval Activity 4

SELF-APPROVAL FOR THE FUTURE

Level: 5 through 8

Subject areas: Language Arts, Social Studies

Directions:

Students learn about various career pathways, which leads to enhanced self-approval. Brainstorm with students about the skills and emotional characteristics a person needs to be effective in these careers.

Pathway	*Specific Careers*
Arts/Communication/ Humanities	actor, graphic designer, prepress & press worker, radio/TV announcer, technical writer, musician, sports broadcaster
Business Systems	accountant, financial clerk, statistician, sales manager, secretary, billing clerk, office manager, business owner
Engineering/ Industrial Systems	architect, autoCAD drafter, carpenter, civil engineer, engineering technician, electrician, programmer
Health Services	dentist, emergency medical technician, licensed practical nurse (LPN), medical laboratory assistant, surgeon, dental hygienist, x-ray technician
Natural Resources	biological scientist, landscaper, environmental analyst, forester, geologist, endangered species surveyor, trails engineer
Social/Human Services	caseworker, firefighter, caterer, teacher, counselor, paralegal, psychologist, camp director, social worker

Self-Approval Activity 4

SELF-APPROVAL FOR THE FUTURE

Level: 2 through 8

Subject areas: Language Arts, Social Studies

Directions:

After students are introduced to the Career Pathways, they need to start comparing their abilities and preferences with the skills needed for the different careers listed. By making these comparisons, students' skills are validated as they see the many career options their skills match. To give students some practice in matching skills to various careers, have them work in teams on this activity. They can study each person's abilities and preferences and then determine the perfect career for each person.

- Charlie is an outgoing and friendly person. He is not very good in sports, and math is always his worst subject. He loves to read and is not shy about getting up in front of people to talk.

Charlie's career should be _____ because

_____.

- John does not enjoy being around people. He enjoys math and computer work. He is not athletic and does not like being outdoors.

John's career should be _____ because

_____.

- Lynda is a good people person, likes a lot of fun and adventure, and enjoys being outside. She has a flair for science, but doesn't do well in math.

Lynda's career should be _____ because

_____.

Self-Approval Activity 4

SELF-APPROVAL FOR THE FUTURE

Level: 2 through 8

Subject areas: Language Arts, Social Studies

Directions:

Now that students have practiced choosing careers for hypothetical individuals based on skills and preferences, it is their turn to choose careers for themselves. They begin by using prior information, such as their abilities and preference lists and the reflection pages. Next, using this information, each student writes a character sketch of himself or herself. Finally, they look at the Career Pathway list to determine the type of career they may be suited for. An example character sketch with a career decision follows.

Character Sketch

I like all outdoor sports. I am also very daring, and this led me to become a dirt bike racer on the weekends. Math and science are my subject strengths, and I am also very mechanically inclined. I enjoy using various tools to fix my dirt bike and have even invented some of my own tools when I couldn't find what I needed.

Career Decision

I am considering becoming a *mechanical engineer* because this career involves a lot of math and science knowledge. This would also be a good career for me because I enjoy mechanics and I like to invent things. As a mechanical engineer, I may even be able to work out-of-doors sometimes.

Through the use of self-approval activities in content lessons, students have opportunities to interpret the curriculum content as it relates to their own actions, beliefs, and feelings. Self-approval starts with self-awareness but moves to a higher level in that people not only gain understanding of their thoughts, feelings, and actions, but they also come to terms with those feelings and behaviors. By fully recognizing that we are who we are, we like what we like, and we feel what we feel, we have opportunities to modify our behaviors and thoughts that are not acceptable to us. When we learn to approve of ourselves, flaws and all, we also learn to accept and embrace the feelings and beliefs of others.

6

Mastering
Self-Responsibility

Learning the arts of self-discipline, self-control, and self-responsibility requires one to be motivated and self-guided. Before individuals can truly master these attributes, they must first be self-aware and have reached self-approval regarding their personal lives (see Figure 6.1).

Self-responsibility means giving up self-centeredness (the "me-first" syndrome) and controlling urges for instant gratification. Amitai Etzioni, a George Washington University social theorist, contends that schools should teach civil education to "develop the knowledge, understandings, and intellectual and participatory skills necessary for competent and responsible citizenship in our constitutional democracy" (Etzioni, Berkowitz, & Wilcox, 1995, p. 6).

What would self-responsibility look like in our students? It would begin before the school bell rings each morning. Students would be responsible for before-school activities such as waking up on time, getting ready for the day, and arriving at school on time and prepared with essential materials needed for the day. Students would think for themselves rather than rely on the teacher or other individuals to do the thinking for them. During the school day, they would assertively ask for assistance when they needed it, but they would also rely on themselves heavily to reason through their own problems. Self-responsible students would keep a daily agenda to stay focused and organized and to make notes of assignment due dates. They would be problem solvers and know how to deal with conflict in a confident manner. They wouldn't make excuses or enter into power struggles with their teachers over class rules or assignments.

FIGURE 6.1. Components of Emotional Intelligence

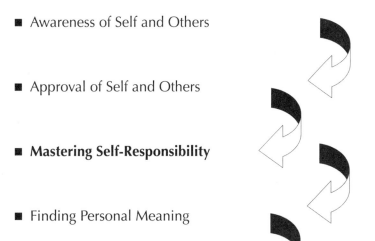

- Awareness of Self and Others

- Approval of Self and Others

- **Mastering Self-Responsibility**

- Finding Personal Meaning

- Valuing Honesty and Ethics

They would accept responsibility for their actions and know how to assertively and appropriately defend their positions if they felt that they had been wronged. Students who have mastered self-responsibility would be in control of their actions, behaviors, consequences, and future destinies. They would understand the natural and logical consequences of their actions, *before* they entered into those actions. A self-responsible student's thought process to demonstrate this understanding might sound similar to the following:

> If I don't turn in my homework on time, I'll lose 25 points. I really can't afford to lose those points, because I didn't score very well on the last test. I'd better make sure I get that work done tonight.

Mastery of self-responsibility enhances emotional intelligence in several ways. First, to see the "big picture" and recognize the logical consequences of one's actions, a person must internalize information and make decisions based on acquired information. This creates a metacognitive thought process that causes individuals to gain understanding of their thoughts and actions.

Second, as students gain skills in self-responsibility, they begin to notice classmates who are not making wise decisions and not demonstrating forethought and understanding of the natural consequences of their actions before they take those actions. The self-responsible, emotionally intelligent students can become peer coaches, as they can empathize with their fellow students' lack of self-responsibility.

Mastering self-responsibility can also lead to less school violence. As students learn techniques to become more responsible learners,

TABLE 6.1 Unit Creation Through Democracy

Unit Plan	Teacher Decision	Student Decision	Both
The class begins a unit on famous inventors.	X		
Students research various inventors and select one inventor to investigate.		X	
Materials are gathered and students begin to take notes on the importance of the invention and inventor.			X
A timeline is set to show due dates of various research components.			X
Students are given a list of expectations regarding content, mechanics, visual aids, and so on.	X		
A performance-based assessment is used, which could be a skit, a narrative, a student-written dialogue, or a replica of the invention.		X	

they also learn suitable ways of responding to various situations and encounters. This includes strategies of anger management, conflict resolution, and emotional safety. Once again, after receiving training in and mastering techniques of self-responsibility, students could work as peer coaches for their fellow classmates who continue to solve problems with inappropriate or aggressive methods.

To facilitate student mastery level of self-responsibility, the classroom adopts a democratic or student-centered approach. This does not imply that students take control and "run the show." A student-centered classroom means students are given choices and have the freedom to make decisions within well-defined limits. This approach is cooperative rather than adversarial. It alleviates many power struggles; as students make decisions and choices, they also learn responsibility. Table 6.1 is an example of how this might occur.

This chart could be used as a new unit is introduced. The teacher and students could list the main components or steps in a particular unit, and democratic decisions could be made regarding the task responsibilities and decisions.

Incorporating the Climate of Democracy

Because our students come from diverse homes, family lifestyles, and backgrounds, the classroom has become the safe and consistent asylum many of our students turn to for their sense of security. Because all children in the United States are required to have an education, our schools should offer a safe place to teach basic life and problem-solving skills that the students may not otherwise learn. These conditions lead to the acute need for educators to provide a safe emotional environment for students.

The incorporation of emotional safety within the classroom requires a structure for a democratic climate. Students not only gain emotional strength when they have input and interaction, they improve their academic performance as well. According to brain researchers Renate and Geoffrey Caine, there are two characteristics for the optimal state of mind in which meaningful learning happens:

1. A relaxed nervous system and a sense of safety and security that operates at mental, emotional, and physical levels

2. Student self-motivation, which is critical to the expansion of knowledge at more than surface levels (Caine & Caine 1994, pp. 83-84)

These two researchers describe a phenomenon they call *relaxed alertness*. This involves a combination of low threat and high challenge. In this classroom atmosphere, students, as well as teachers, feel safe enough to explore learning techniques, search for information, express thoughts and opinions, and demonstrate learning through atypical and innovative means. By contrast, this classroom environment also requires high teacher and student expectations, challenging curriculum, and engaged learning.

When the school year begins, many teachers pass out the classroom rules and procedures and advise students of the consequences if these procedures are not followed. Although setting clear expectations is an important component in developing the classroom climate, by handing out your rules, they become just that—*your* rules. In a democratic classroom, students have input (not control) regarding the routine, procedures, and rules. Teachers and students together determine if the recommended rules are rules that they can "live with." Obviously, if students decide they want a 2-hour recess every day, that isn't feasible and is not something a teacher could live with. But given the chance, students often suggest very structured guidelines that are reasonable and fair. Encourage students to include emotional safety issues, such as a No Fear plan, as they brainstorm class guidelines. In a No Fear plan, students decide what they need from their peers to feel safe and unafraid in the classroom.

The physical atmosphere of the democratic classroom offers choices as well. There may be various centers around the room to choose from, a book corner with a wide array of interesting materials, or perhaps a listening center for students who need some personal time. Student work is displayed and nonthreatening creativity stations are available for student free time.

After the classroom environment has been established, procedures should be posted and practiced daily. Students need the safety of knowing the expectations and routine. By rehearsing the agreed-on procedures and working in a safe, yet challenging, environment, students begin to feel they are a very important part of the learning process, which is the introductory step in self-responsibility.

Internalizing Information for Making Appropriate Choices

An extremely effective teaching tool for both academic and emotional gains involves "thinking about thinking," or *metacognition.* This tool may be implemented in the beginning, middle, or end of a lesson. Let's say a science teacher hands students a bag of objects from nature. The bag may contain leaves, stones, flowers, twigs, bones, and so on. The teacher asks the students to decide on a strategy for classifying these objects. As students are completing the classification activity, the teacher stops the class and asks, "How did your group decide on a method for classification? How did you feel about your classification system? How might you classify these items differently the next time?"

By thinking directly about their thought processes, students are much more likely to internalize the information and transfer the new knowledge into long-term memory. They are also learning a sense of responsibility as they are asked to think about the decisions they made and determine whether their decisions make sense. When students are asked to think metacognitively often enough, they begin to learn more in depth because they recognize and capitalize on their personal strengths while improving or allowing for weaknesses (Caine & Caine, 1994).

Overt reflective thinking would be a natural next step in the metacognitive process. For an optimal learning experience, this same science teacher would ask students to write a journal entry about the lesson. The teacher would ask for the topic, the objective, the processes followed, and the results. More important, the teacher would ask for students to write down their thought processes throughout the lesson. The writings might even include the personal frustrations and stumbling blocks that kept individual students from successful learning experiences.

As students are prompted to internalize information and think reflectively, they begin to take responsibility for their own learning and academic growth. In addition, they investigate an avenue that promotes emotional growth and maturity.

Understanding Natural Consequences

Natural consequences are events that follow naturally after an incident or situation. They place the responsibility on the student, rather than on the teacher, because the student is receiving an outcome based on his or her own actions. An example follows.

Timmy: Mr. Underwood, you are going to be sooooo mad at me.

It was difficult to ever feel annoyed at Timmy with his friendly disposition, shining blue eyes, and bright smile.

Mr. Underwood: Oh, I doubt that I'll be mad at you, Timmy. What is it?

Timmy: Well, I sort of forgot the Native American research information on the kitchen table last night.

Mr. Underwood: Very well, Timmy. You forgot your homework.

Timmy: Yeah, but it was due today. And since it's a cooperative project, my group was depending on me. Aren't you mad at me?

Mr. Underwood: Of course not. How could I be mad at you, Timmy?

Timmy: Oh, good! So, I can just bring it in tomorrow?

Mr. Underwood: Well, since your group can't move any further until you have your part of the research, bringing it tomorrow wouldn't work. What a lucky break for you that we aren't working on Social Studies until *after* lunch!!!

Timmy: So, you mean I have to look up information during lunch when I already have it done at home?

Mr. Underwood: Well, Timmy, you decide what you need to do. All I can tell you is that your group needs that information today.

The teacher's role regarding natural consequences is one of very little involvement. In fact, many teachers have to fight with themselves to maintain a background position rather than making a take-charge, "I told you so," assertion. If the teacher has involved students in developing class procedures and expectations, then it should be very clear to students what the natural consequence of an

TABLE 6.2 Situation and Natural Consequence

Situation	Natural Consequence
Students misuse art supplies and now they are all damaged or lost.	Do not replace art supplies until students are experiencing sufficient loss with regard to art activities.
Students forget their lunches every day and have to call their parents to bring lunch to them.	Have conferences with the students' parents and the students ahead of time. Agree that the next time the students forget lunch, they will have the natural consequence of not having lunch.
Students continually forget their homework.	The natural consequence could be a failed grade, no recess until the homework is done, or staying after school each day until the student catches up.
Students turn in such sloppy work the teacher can't read it.	The teacher could pass the work back to the students and say, "I'll be glad to grade this when it is written neatly enough to be read."
Students forget their props or costumes for the play.	"The show must go on," and these students will have to wear their regular school attire during the performance.
Children aren't responsible with their personal hygiene and have body odor.	Other students won't want to sit by these students and peer pressure will come into play.
Students procrastinate and don't prepare for oral presentations.	The teacher might say, "This is the day we are doing oral presentations. You may choose to take a zero, or you may attempt to present whatever information you have."
Children become angry or violent during a school baseball game.	Because these behaviors are not acceptable according to the procedures outlined by the school, these children are not welcome to play baseball at school without first having anger-management coaching.

action is, should they make a choice to not follow these procedures. When students are in a situation that concludes with natural consequences without the children's being in danger, it is crucial for the development of self-responsibility that teachers limit their involvement. Mr. Underwood never had to raise his voice with Timmy. He never had to give Timmy an ultimatum. He very calmly and sequentially spelled out the need for Timmy's completed information and let the natural consequence take its course. Table 6.2 lists some other situations that call for natural consequences.

Students who consistently learn natural consequences the hard way may benefit from peer coaching or peer tutoring. The teacher may want to choose student coaches who are already very responsible or students who need to practice their own social skills. For example, the following peer coaching and mentoring methods might be used to address the situations listed in Table 6.2.

▶ Peer coaches could be assigned to help children who forget their lunch money every day. The coaches would remind the forgetful students once a day consistently for the first week and then intermittently the next week. The coaches would not assume responsibility for making sure these children had lunch but would serve as interim support as the forgetful children developed new habits.

▶ When students continually forget their homework, even though they experience the natural consequence of no recess, they may benefit from peer coaching. The student coaches could call the forgetful students each evening for the first week to remind them to bring in their homework. The following week, the phone calls would be intermittent, and eventually, the forgetful students would be expected to develop their new behavior of bringing homework to school each day.

▶ A peer tutor might be effective in the case of students turning in sloppy assignment papers. Tutors would sit next to the students in need. As assignments are worked on, the tutor could demonstrate some organization strategies and neatness techniques that would benefit the other children. Again, a weaning process would take place, during which the tutor would gradually expect the student being tutored to demonstrate self-responsibility.

▶ We've all had students in our classrooms who are not self-aware regarding personal hygiene. Rather than put students on the spot by asking them to take on the role of peer coach, this situation would be better resolved through adult intervention. This could mean a one-on-one talk with the child, a discussion with the parents, or the involvement of another adult the child trusts a good deal. The main point of this intervention would be the how-to's of self-responsibility in personal hygiene.

▶ Regarding the angry or violent child who erupted during a school baseball game, the consequences fit the behavior. The school or baseball coach has set clear expectations with students regarding appropriate behaviors while they are involved with this sport. Obviously, this child did not abide by the expected rules for behavior, and a natural consequence is exclusion from future games until anger management coaching has taken place.

Natural consequences provide meaningful learning situations for our students. Rather than the teacher or parent taking responsibility for the child's actions, students themselves are in control of the situation. Rules and procedures may have been put in place by teachers initially, but natural consequences put the ball back in the students' court.

Self-Responsibility Regarding School Violence

Violence has found its way inside the classroom doors. Although currently our classrooms still provide one of the safest atmospheres possible for our youth, there is cause for concern. To foster safe and secure schools, classroom teachers must take preventive measures for the mental and emotional well-being of the children. Entire schools and school districts must assume responsibility for creating intervention programs to foster school safety. Focus must be placed on early warning signs and children at risk of committing violent acts. And most important, students themselves must take part in the development and implementation of intervention and prevention programs. From the beginning of their school years, students must be taught to take responsibility for their actions and about the natural and consistent consequences of their actions.

Research shows that effective schools communicate the attitude that all children can achieve academically and behave appropriately, while at the same time, individual differences can be appreciated (Haynes, Comer, & Hamilton-Lee, 1988). This message is conveyed with adequate resources and programs that set consistent expectations. In these expectations, it is clearly stated to students that they are an integral component in the entire school safety process. They are responsible for their actions, behaviors, and attitudes, and they are aware of the natural consequences for those who do not participate in the violence prevention strategies.

Our students come to school with many different perceptions, attitudes, and views regarding violence, hate, death, and weapons. By discussing these issues and their natural consequences openly with our students, we may reduce the risk of violence. Teachers can incorporate discussions on firearms and the responsibilities of owning a firearm. After reading articles, literature studies, and science or social studies materials, the class can debate and discuss the self-responsibility or lack of responsibility they notice in the various characters in their readings.

Finally, to instill self-responsibility for the development of non-violent behaviors, the classroom teacher must allow students to share their concerns about current local incidents, school conflicts, or personal conflicts in their lives.

When a conflict arises in the classroom, what better way to teach nonviolent solutions than to take the class through these problem-solving steps to determine an appropriate response? Students must learn all the basic steps of problem solving for future use and have opportunities to practice these steps. The four steps to problem solving are the following:

1. State the problem.

2. Brainstorm for all possible solutions.

3. Narrow down the choices by taking out unworkable solutions.

4. Choose one best solution or a combination of best solutions.

Academic Self-Responsibility

In current school systems in the United States, some students still fall through the academic cracks. Student populations in schools and in each classroom have become so large that students do not benefit as much from academic instruction as they could. Teachers are under pressure to *do something to bring up student test scores and do it quickly*. There is little time to focus on the importance of student responsibility regarding academic success; yet this may be the very key that educators are looking for.

When children find a way to avoid responsibility, for example, by not completing a homework assignment, they can easily turn this behavior into a pattern. After all, why would a student choose to spend hours of hard work on a project, when there are no consequences for *not* turning in the assignment? When this pattern is established, the behavior is not likely to change until some accountability is built into the system (Mackenzie, 1996). A procedure needs to be established for monitoring the student's assignment completion, and follow-through with logical consequences must be maintained. Consistency with procedures and logical consequences not only increases student opportunities for academic success but also gives the child the security of a democratic classroom environment.

Students also must have frequent opportunities to reflect on the content they are learning and how it affects them personally. If they aren't able to find meaningful connections between the concepts and their personal lives, perhaps teachers could give guidance in finding those connections.

In addition to consistent procedures as a means of producing academic self-responsibility, students must feel a "buy-in" toward the learned material. They must sense the purpose of the material they are studying and a relevant connection to their own interests and emotions.

To engage a student in the learning process and thereby induce academic responsibility, curriculum expectations should build on children's personal interests and motivations. Children must be empowered to engage meaningfully in their own learning (Gardner, 1993). If they have opportunities to explore relevant content areas in depth, students feel more responsibility in the learning.

Assessment should have the same criteria as the learning process. When students are actively engaged in a performance assessment, they are more apt to feel intrinsically motivated in the communication of their knowledge. Such types of performance assessments could include the following activities:

■ Group presentations

■ Portfolio presentations (accumulated unit assignments)

■ Skits (accumulated unit information in student-written skits)

■ Overhead transparency demonstrations

■ Collages (accumulated visual projects from unit)

■ Reflection essays about content learned and its relevance to the learners

In a classroom set up for academic self-responsibility, students would still receive basic lessons in English, math, reading, science, and social studies. In addition to these lessons, students would also be immersed in extended studies of these subjects involving topics of special interest to them. They would all be aware of academic expectations and the logical consequences should they choose not to participate fully. They would have periodic chances to reflect metacognitively about what they were studying. And finally, in the culminating project, they would share with others what they had learned in the content, emotional, and introspective realms of their studies.

When students are allowed to find meaningful connections to learning and are given opportunities to reflect on learning and how it affects them, they are more apt to feel a sense of responsibility in the learning process. In addition, by knowing the expectations for learning and the natural consequences for not living up to those expectations, students are adding a new dimension to their understanding of self-responsibility. Several suggested activities follow for use with students to help them increase self-responsibility skills.

For the teacher, fostering self-responsibility in students means embracing a democratic style of teaching. It also means creating an environment of "relaxed alertness," where students are sufficiently challenged, yet safe and secure. Students receive information and become decision makers based on the presented information. They learn to rely on themselves and accept responsibility for their errors. These students are in control of their daily actions and behaviors as well as their future destinies.

Self-Responsibility Activity 1

NATURAL CONSEQUENCES

Level: K through 4

Subject areas: Language Arts, Social Studies

Directions:
Natural consequences shouldn't be secrets only the teacher is privy to. Students can learn about natural consequences through social studies or language arts content. This allows students to determine the logical and natural consequences following actions. Examples are listed below.

Action: George Washington chopped down the cherry tree.

Consequence: He had to earn back his father's trust.

Action: Pocahontas helped the white settlers plant corn.

Consequence:

_____

Action: Sleeping Beauty pricked her finger on the spinning wheel.

Consequence:

_____

Self-Responsibility Activity 1

NATURAL CONSEQUENCES

Level: 5 through 8

Subject areas: Language Arts, Social Studies

Directions:
Natural consequences shouldn't be secrets only the teacher is privy to. Students can learn about natural consequences through social studies or language arts content. This allows students to determine the logical and natural consequences following actions. Examples are listed below.

Action: The Emancipation Proclamation was signed.

Consequence:

_____

Action: Abraham Lincoln gave his Gettysburg Address speech.

Consequence:

_____

Action: The Declaration of Independence was signed.

Consequence:

_____

Action: The Triangular Trade was established.

Consequence:

_____

Self-Responsibility Activity 1

NATURAL CONSEQUENCES

Level: 5 through 8 (Continued)

Action: Bartolomeu Dias sailed around the tip of Africa.

Consequence:

_____

Action: Gold was discovered in California.

Consequence:

_____

Action: Queen Isabella agreed to let Columbus set sail.

Consequence:

_____

Action: An assassin killed Dr. Martin Luther King Jr.

Consequence:

_____

Self-Responsibility Activity 2

ACADEMIC SELF-RESPONSIBILITY

Level: K through 4

Subject areas: All

Directions:

Students should periodically reflect on their academic strengths and weaknesses. This activity provides a worksheet to begin the reflection process.

Kindergarten through 2nd-grade teachers may need to guide students orally through this process.

Academic Strength	*Academic Weakness*
Draw the ways that you are smart.	Draw the things in school that are hard for you.

How can this strength get even stronger?	How can this weakness be improved?

Illustrate ways that you might use these skills in the future.

Self-Responsibility Activity 2

ACADEMIC SELF-RESPONSIBILITY

Level: 5 through 8

Subject areas: All

Directions:

Students should periodically reflect on their academic strengths and weaknesses. This activity provides a worksheet to begin the reflection process.

Academic Strength	Academic Weakness
List two academic strengths.	List two academic weaknesses.

Specifically, *how* are these subjects strengths or weaknesses?

How can you enhance this strength to be stronger?	How can you improve this weakness?

Describe incidents or events where you might need these skills

Self-Responsibility Activity 3

MAKING GOOD CHOICES

Level: K through 4

Subject areas: All

Directions:

Students need a structure to use in solving real problems. They also need opportunities to practice the appropriate solutions and responses.

Read the following story to students. Then follow the problem-solving steps to a final decision. The culminating activity should be a class discussion about student emotional reactions, the actions of the boy in the story, and the solutions the students choose for him.

The Third-Grade Dilemma

In Mrs. Hartley's third-grade classroom, the students were diligently working on a play based on *Jack and the Beanstalk*. During rehearsal one day, Jonny, who was playing the part of Jack, had a mishap. He was climbing down the imaginary beanstalk, which was really a rope covered in vines, when he fell off the chair and landed in a heap on the floor. When the other children saw that Jonny was all right, they began to laugh at the comical position he had landed in. The laughter got louder and louder. Jonny began to get angrier and angrier. He finally stood up and started swinging wildly at anyone who was within reach. The students stopped laughing and started running away from Jonny, who was by now quite enraged with the whole situation.

Problem Solving

The main problem in this story is _____

_____

_____

_____

Self-Responsibility Activity 3

MAKING GOOD CHOICES

Level: K through 4 (Continued)

Some good solutions to this problem are _____

_____

_____

_____

_____

The three solutions that would work best are _____

_____

_____

_____

We agree that the overall best solution to this problem is _____

_____

_____

_____

Self-Responsibility Activity 3

MAKING GOOD CHOICES

Level: 5 through 8

Subject areas: All

Directions:

Students need a structure to use in solving real problems. They also need opportunities to practice appropriate solutions and responses. Read the following story to students. Then follow the problem-solving steps toward finding a workable solution. Students should eventually use these steps in cooperative groups and individually. Problem solving should be followed by discussion and sharing ideas.

Freedom of Choice

Everyone knew Donna was a problem at school. She exasperated the teachers, the students, and the administration with her loud and obnoxious opinions. During civics class one day, students were discussing freedom of choice. One shy boy, Tony, ventured to voice his opinion. He explained that in the United States, we have the opportunity to get the kind of education we want, choose the kind of job we want, and choose a spouse who suits us. Donna took this opportunity to pounce on Tony. She hooted loudly and proceeded to tell him he didn't need to worry about getting a spouse with his zit face and greasy hair. She told him that because he was so big on freedom of choice, maybe he had better choose to bury his head in the sand so nobody would have to look at it.

Something happened next nobody expected. Shy Tony jumped up out of his seat with fire in his eyes. He lunged at Donna with both hands and pushed her as hard as he could. Donna flew from her seat onto the floor. This was a new experience for Donna, as nobody ever challenged her! Angry and humiliated, Donna jumped up and declared war. Before the teacher was able to move, Tony and Donna were in a full-blown fistfight, right in the middle of the classroom.

Problem Solving

State the main problem.

Self-Responsibility Activity 3

MAKING GOOD CHOICES

Level: 5 through 8 (Continued)

What do we know about the problem?

_____

What do we need to know?

_____

Where can we go for information?

_____

Brainstorm for all possible solutions.

_____

_____

_____

_____

_____

Decide on one best final solution (or combine two solutions).

_____

_____

_____

_____

Be ready to share your solution and the methods that your team used to reach the solution.

Self-Responsibility Activity 4

FROM SCHOOL TO JOB

Level: K through 8

Subject areas: All

Directions:

Students brainstorm a list of all the ways school is similar to a job and the ways it is different from a job. Use a Venn diagram or other graphic organizer to show comparison results.

Kindergarten through 2nd-grade students may show similarities through a mural painting.

How School Is Like a Job

	School	*Job*
Regarding homework		
Regarding being reliable		
Regarding time		
Regarding money		
Regarding skills		
Regarding following rules		
Regarding peers		

7

Finding Personal Meaning

Children are seekers of meaning. No sooner do they learn how to talk than they begin asking questions about simple things as well as about dilemmas of human existence that have perplexed philosophers and theologians since the dawn of time. Children are intensely interested in exploring questions of values, feelings, meaning, and the relationship of self to others.

—California Department of Education,
Elementary Task Force Report:
It's Elementary!

Students must be able to construe relevant meanings and connections for the learned information to become committed to long-term memory. They must feel an emotional tie to the information and must find patterns in the learning that make sense to them. Lessons in the classroom must provide opportunities for students to find those connections, those ties, and those patterns for optimal learning to occur. By finding personal meaning in a piece of information, students find self-worth and self-acceptance in that they become an integral component in the learning process (see Figure 7.1).

FIGURE 7.1. Components of Emotional Intelligence

■ Awareness of Self and Others

■ Approval of Self and Others

■ Mastering Self-Responsibility

■ **Finding Personal Meaning**

■ Valuing Honesty and Ethics

Because all three layers of the brain—the reptilian brain, the limbic system, and the neocortex—are continuously interacting with each other, we know that **concepts + emotions + responses** are all interrelated in the learning process (Caine & Caine, 1994).

The limbic system (see Figure 7.2) houses both emotion and memory, so it would only stand to reason that an emotional impact regarding a thought would trigger a long-term memory (Caine & Caine, 1994). It is a fact that our students are feeling, perceiving, constructing meaning, and reflecting each and every day. It is our job to tailor the curriculum and instructional techniques so these processes occur while they are learning content information.

An ideal teaching method allowing students to find deep meaning involves an explorative study. The teacher supplies the background content information regarding a particular topic, and then students choose a certain aspect of that study to explore, research, and examine. The students are encouraged to use multiple-intelligence media to produce a final product to share. This means they may construct a 3-dimensional project (bodily/kinesthetic), or they may write a song (musical/rhythmical). Verbal/linguistic students may choose to create a skit or speech, and visual/spatial students may draw or paint their product. The final project is put on display and presented to the class with an in-depth discussion about the topic. A final component to the project would be a reflection journal in which students would use metacognitive thought processes about what they learned, how they felt about their learning, what they wish they had researched in greater depth, and so on.

FIGURE 7.2. The Limbic System

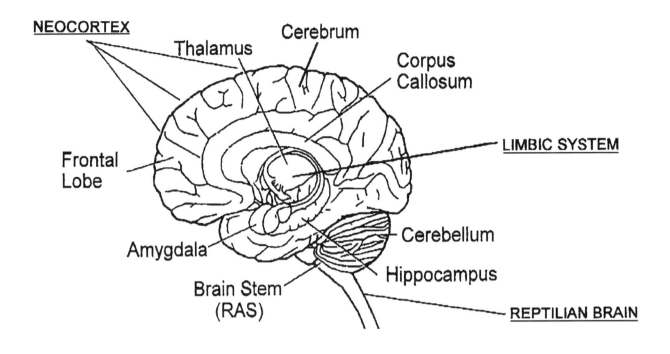

In their book, *Making Connections: Teaching and the Human Brain*, Geoffrey and Renate Caine (1994) demonstrate the concepts of *route learning* and *map learning*. When teachers use traditional strategies, such as those that follow, they are using a route-learning approach.

1. Introduce a new concept to students.

2. Assign practice work to check for understanding.

3. Review practice work.

4. Test students for understanding.

The content, objectives, and teaching strategies were predetermined by the teacher with definite expected outcomes from students. The testing accommodating a route-learning approach includes multiple-choice, true-false, or fill-in-the-blank tests. Because student contributions and feedback were not solicited regarding the learning, students are limited to cognitive surface gains and not in-depth meaning.

By contrast, when teachers use map-learning methods, a concept might be taught with these steps:

1. Teacher introduces a thematic topic.

2. Each student chooses a particular area of that topic in which he or she will become an expert.

3. Students research their topics and create projects that demonstrate their understanding of the topics.

4. Students present their projects as their performance assessments.

Learning through map processing is much more meaningful and motivating to the student than route learning. Because it is personally relevant to students, their chances of transferring this information to long-term memory greatly increase.

Although the map-learning approach shows undeniable benefits, in the real world of education with state standards to adhere to and district curricula to labor through, it is not always possible to use map-learning strategies. And there are occasions when students need to learn information that is best taught through the route approach. We use route methods when we want students to learn specific information, such as the names of the parts of the body or the state capitals. However, even with lessons involving straight memorization, we can incorporate some teaching strategies to create meaning for students. For instance, in learning the parts of the body, students can choose three parts of the body and do a short study on how these three parts are interdependent with each other. In memorizing state capitals, students could write about an imaginary trip around the country, and as they reach each state, they describe the environment they observe as they visit the state capital.

We know that route learning takes less time, is easier preparation for the teacher, and gives measurable results, but research shows unquestionably that students gain deeper understanding of concepts through a map approach. It is vital that educators realize the impact on learning we can have by teaching in a meaningful context.

Brain Changes

What is actually happening in the brain when students gain meaningful knowledge? What proof do we have that engaging our students in interactive learning is actually more beneficial to them? To answer these questions, let's look at a UCLA study conducted in 1964. Mark Rosenzweig wanted to determine whether the physical structure of the brain changed and expanded as a result of stimulation, experience, and a positive environment. Three groups of rats were used as the subjects of this experiment.

■ Group 1 rats lived in a visually and physically stimulating environment (cage full of wheels, ladders, toys, mazes, and so on).

■ Group 2 rats lived in an impoverished atmosphere with no stimulation whatsoever.

■ Group 3 rats could see the exciting life of Group 1 animals, but were somewhat impoverished as they had no physical stimulation.

In examining the brains of these three rat groups, those who had direct interaction in a challenging environment had actually developed a much heavier and thicker cerebral cortex than the other two groups of rats. Enzymes found in glial cells changed by 10%, and the total number of glia increased by 14%. Glia cells are critical to brain functioning because they provide food for the brain cells that transmit signals. The experiment demonstrates that when individuals are directly involved with mental stimulation and can engage in new ideas and experiences, knowledge and meaning are enhanced. In short, meaningful interactions and experiences truly shape the physical structure of our brain, and, therefore, shape our future learning (Bennett, Diamond, Krech, & Rosenzweig, 1964).

The 4 Ms

Students who can see the relevance of what they are learning and who develop a connection with the learned material develop feelings of self-worth and pride. When demonstrating their knowledge through a performance assessment rather than a route assessment, students also gain new meaning through the assessment, and learn valuable tools for emotional intelligence. This happens as they receive specific and positive feedback from peers and teachers and because during the presentation of learned material, students become cognitively aware of the knowledge they have gained, which enhances self-esteem. To ensure that methods for invoking meaningful learning are truly working, instructors can use the 4 Ms in their lesson planning: *meaningful material, motivation, movement, and multiple intelligences.*

Meaningful Material

When a content topic is presented to students, the teaching methods must be complex, lifelike, and integrated for students to achieve deep meaning. Thorough understanding happens when the learner is challenged by intellect, creativity, and emotions. Students must have an opinion or a *feeling* about the material, and lessons must be presented to elicit those emotions. As previously discussed, content becomes relevant and meaningful to students when they "own" it. This implies that students must be involved in the decision-making process to determine components of the topic they will research, methods they will use to research the topic, and how they will demonstrate their knowledge of the topic. The democratic classroom comes into play here. For material to be truly meaningful to students, teachers have to be willing to let go of the authority enough to allow students to feel meaning in their own way, explore meaning through various alternatives, and provide knowledge through nontraditional methods. However, it must be made clear that to provide students with options or stimulating activities is not enough. For deep meaning to occur, students need objectives in mind that *make sense to them* as they go on their exploration mission. This is true whether the lesson involves the whole class or just individuals; students need to know the purpose of what they are learning. Once this has been established, a multitude of strategies are available to enhance the learning process. Examples of meaningful strategies include the following:

► *Cooperative learning* usually involves groups of four students each. In a cooperative-learning situation, students may work as a team to solve a problem, make a decision, discuss the meaning of information, or share opinions about a topic. They may also each be responsible for becoming an expert on a piece of the whole concept. Let's say, for example, that students must create a project about the Old West. They are expected to show knowledge of events leading to westward migration, careers of the Old West, culture (food, clothing, dance, etc.), and famous people of the Old West. Each team member chooses one component and becomes an expert in that piece. After all team members have accumulated material, they decide how to create a project to demonstrate their knowledge.

► *Authentic learning* enables students to see the relevance of what they are learning to real life so they can make connections and develop a keener sense of how the information has meaning for them. To give students a feeling for the efforts of the Egyptians in building the pyramids, students might first learn background information. They would watch videos, read articles, and perhaps visit a museum or have a guest speaker explain the amount of work involved in these magnificent buildings. Next, students would get involved in the actual construction of a pyramid, using the same techniques the Egyptians used. They would have a much clearer understanding of Egyptian architecture at the end of this project because they were authentically involved in the building process.

▶ *Thematic learning* is based on the premise that students become more absorbed in the learning if they are involved in a theme rather than working with isolated subjects throughout the day. For instance, in a thematic unit about pollution, subject areas could be covered in the following ways:

1. Language Arts—Begin the unit by reading the Dr. Seuss book, *The Wump World*. This is followed by discussion and reflection related to the catastrophes pollution can cause.

2. Language Arts—Read about water, air, and noise pollution from a variety of sources, including newspaper articles, magazines, books, Web sites, and so on.

3. Math and Science—Research the different geographical areas of the world, classifying them as high-pollution areas, mid-range pollution areas, or low pollution areas. Next, graph the pollution levels according to these findings.

4. Math and Science—Test local lake or stream water to find the pollution levels. Determine what category these samples would fall under.

5. Social Studies—Choose early pioneers of environmental awareness and make a timeline to show a sequence of dates of environmental accomplishments.

6. Language Arts—Work in cooperative groups to solve existing pollution problems, and then write letters to members of Congress to express concerns and solutions.

7. Culminating Event—Visit a water treatment plant, airport, or environmental control laboratory to discover some of the current pollution control devices being used.

8. Culminating Event—Create a project to be shared orally to demonstrate student knowledge and awareness of pollution and possible solutions to this problem.

Motivation

Extrinsic motivation involves gratification that occurs outside a child's psyche. This gratification can be in the form of a good grade on an assignment or a tangible reward such as a sticker on a test or a star on a classroom chart. Extrinsic motivation is necessary when students have not developed an interest in or internal purpose for learning the information being presented. Although this method of motivation occurs frequently, it does not lead to emotional intelligence because it does not give a child a deep sense of understanding, a sense of purpose, or the type of feedback that leads to self-approval.

In a spelling lesson, a teacher may dole out the list of words students are expected to study for the week. Perhaps all students complete the daily activities of writing the words in a sentence, practicing the words with a partner, or copying the words three times each. Some of the students take their lists home and study for the test because they are extrinsically motivated to get an A on the test. Perhaps the overall spelling test scores are even high in a particular classroom using these strategies. The problem lies in the fact that students who are performing only for extrinsic rewards are not learning for the long term. This type of teaching does not involve meaningful connections, and it is very unlikely that students transfer these words into long-term memory.

Intrinsic motivation, on the other hand, involves learning through curiosity, interest, excitement, or novelty. Students are engaged in activities that have sparked a personal interest. They care about the information they are learning and are inspired to pursue a more in-depth study of the topic.

Let's take the spelling lesson example and turn the extrinsic motivation into an intrinsic one. In this classroom, students are involved in a literature study. Each day, they read a section of the book and then engage in activities centered on the book's contents. On Monday morning, the teacher tells the students the approximate number of pages they may be reading for that week. Students then skim through those pages looking for words they aren't familiar with. They write down the words and the words in context. From the student-generated lists of words, the class decides on a group of words they will study that week. Students work in pairs to read a word in context from the story, and then use a dictionary to look the word up. They look for dictionary definitions that seem to fit with the word in context. Next, they write those definitions in their own words as they fit with the word in context. They continue in this pattern until they have defined all the words. They now feel some ownership of their chosen words and their meanings.

On Tuesday, students review their word lists and definitions. They talk about and practice the spelling of the words as they define them. During the reading lesson, they come to these words and once again have the opportunity to review and discuss their meanings and spelling. They achieve an even deeper meaning now that they have read more of the story that leads up to the words. By Friday, most students feel a true connection to the words and can spell, define, and write the words in sentence context. Students have been motivated intrinsically, and there was no need for stickers, the threat of a test, or any other external component.

Movement

Carla Hannaford, Howard Gardner, Maria Montessori, Jean Ayres, Neil Kephardt, and other learning specialists all agree that movement is crucial to the learning process. Abilities to act out a mime sequence, create a dance, play a game, or create an invention are all evidence of the cognitive factors of body usage (Gardner, 1993). Effective processing happens when all aspects of the brain are addressed; this includes stimulation during active interaction as well as powerful engagement of the emotions. Students must become active participants in learning rather than passive listeners in a classroom. This is not to imply that students must be physically jumping around to gain a true understanding of the curriculum. But for a thought to occur, there must be movement. Even though a person may be sitting perfectly still, some kind of movement must occur for that thought to be maintained. This movement could be a very overt action such as a game of charades, or it may be as simple as writing that thought down on paper.

An important factor for educators to understand is that individual students may need varying amounts of movement. Some of our children may actually need to pace the floor as a means of processing information, and we must be flexible enough to allow it. To ensure time on task with few disruptions, teachers and students may actually generate a list of acceptable and unacceptable movements.

Multiple Intelligences

Howard Gardner (1993) has identified eight attributes that qualify as actual intelligences. Although individuals are born with a predisposition toward intellectual strengths and weaknesses, research shows that effective teaching strategies and enriching environments can lead to increased intelligences. When students have opportunities to increase their intellectual abilities, they also increase their emotional intelligence. Examples of Howard Gardner's multiple intelligences with activities for enhancement include the following (Gardner, 1993):

Verbal/Linguistic

- Student debates
- Petitions
- Advertisements
- Comic strips
- Demonstrations
- Journaling
- Simulated TV or talk radio
- Editorial essays

Logical/Mathematical

- Mazes
- Categorized collections
- Charts and graphs
- Computer programs
- Timelines
- Problem solving
- Experiments
- Sequencing

Visual/Spatial

- Painting
- Prototypes
- Murals, collages, models
- Animated movies
- Dioramas, mobiles, pop-up books
- Making games
- Illustrating stories
- Travel brochures

Bodily/Kinesthetic

- Role-playing
- Papier mâché
- Press conferences
- Experimenting
- Dance, making costumes, performing
- Filming/movie making
- Pantomime
- Radio/TV show
- Sports

Musical/Rhythmical

- Lyrics or melodies
- Poems
- Tape recordings
- Nature sounds
- Instrumental music
- Listening to music on headsets during independent work
- Riddles
- Rhymes

Interpersonal

- Plays
- Cooperative learning
- Partner sharing
- Discussions
- Advertisements
- Group presentations
- Press conferences
- Demonstrations
- Feedback

Intrapersonal

- Journaling
- Poems
- Self-reflection
- Collections
- Personal narratives
- Drawings
- Guided imagery
- Diaries
- Painting

Naturalist

- Nature walks
- Nature music
- Map making
- Investigating/exploring
- Writing observations
- Making discoveries
- Animal lessons
- Environmental studies
- Global discussions

Remembering that **concepts + emotions + responses** are all interrelated in the learning process, the 4 Ms give instructors tools for achieving higher student interaction that can result in higher academic learning.

Using the 4 Ms would create an emotional impact regarding a thought that triggers a long-term memory. It is a fact that our students are feeling, perceiving, constructing meaning, and reflecting each and every day. By using the 4 Ms in our curriculum, we can increase opportunities for students to develop personal meanings for the presented material.

The following activities are intended to enhance students' abilities to find personal meaning in assigned activities.

(text continues on page 113)

Personal Meaning Activity 1

NEWSPAPER STUDIES

Level: K through 4

Subject areas: Language Arts, Social Studies, Science

Directions:
Each pair of students is given a copy of a local newspaper. Sample activities involving personal meaning are as follows:

- After looking at the comics section of the newspaper, students cut out their favorite comic strip, mix it up, and then glue it to tagboard in the correct sequential order.

- After learning letter recognition and letter sounds, students cut out these letters from the paper.

- After learning the hard and soft sounds of C or G, students cut out words that begin with one of these letters and then glue them onto a board in the correct category, such as soft G sound and hard G sound.

- Look at the weather map in the newspaper. Students learn some of the weather symbols and then create their own symbols to show weather events. After receiving a blank United States map, they can make a key with their new symbols and show current weather trends over the next few days.

Personal Meaning Activity 1

NEWSPAPER STUDIES

Level: 5 through 8

Subject areas: Language Arts, Social Studies, Math

Directions:

Each cooperative group receives a copy of the local newspaper. Suggested activities for teaching personal meaning include the following:

- Students read an article of interest to them. They then cut out and paste on paper and board:
  - The topic sentence
  - Five important detail sentences in sequential order

- Students read and discuss the editorial section of the newspaper. Then each team member writes a letter to the editor on a topic about which they have a strong opinion.

- Students choose an article from the sports section of the paper. After reading and reflecting on the article, they write the "who, what, where, when, and why" of their articles. Next, they write their own sports article, making sure to include these same five Ws in their own article.

- Using the weather section of the paper, students record temperatures from various geographical locations and graph them. They then compare their own geographical area with others to determine overall weather differences in the United States.

- After becoming familiar with the different sections of the paper, students write a class newspaper. They choose the section they want to work on. Section choices may include front page, sports, editorial, comics, classifieds, and so on. Each group of four or five students is responsible for writing five articles for their section. Each team decides on the articles they write about and the resources and materials they need. Then, they edit each other's work as articles are completed.

Personal Meaning Activity 2

MULTIPLE STRATEGIES FOR PERSONAL MEANING

Level: K through 8

Subject areas: All

The following list contains teaching practices and activities that enhance personal meaning, and learning opportunities for students.

K–8   Individual Growth Learning. Students incorporate their own family history, hobbies, or experiences into their learning projects to create higher interest and deeper meaning.

3–8   *Student-Made Games.* After a unit study, students use the learned information to create board games. They are then given an afternoon to play each other's games.

3–8   *Group Presentations.* Students work as a team to present learned information in an interesting way.

1–8   *Learning Centers.* When centers offer some student choices, they can become very meaningful additions to the learning process.

3–8   *Thematic Instruction.* This method of instruction allows for the patterns and connections to be established for the learner.

4–8   *Debates.* Students are asked to choose sides on any current subject. They research and study in preparation for the debate, and make a case for their cause.

K–8   *Physical Creations.* When students can create a project such as a replica, model, poster, diorama, or diagram, the chances for a meaningful learning experience are greatly increased.

3–8   *Role-Playing.* After completing a literature study or a historical unit, students choose roles and act out the parts (thus implanting information in long-term memory).

K–8   *Reflection.* Students need opportunities to reflect on how the learned material is meaningful to them. This could be done through class discussion, journaling, partner team talk, or cooperative groups.

Summary

Because the brain is always searching for connections and patterns to create meaning (Caine & Caine, 1994), our lesson plans and teaching practices must include components that enhance personal meaning for students. Students may construct emotional meaning (e.g., understanding and implementing nonviolent methods of solving conflict), or intellectual meaning (e.g., transferring vocabulary understanding into long-term memory because the words were relevant to the student).

As lesson plans are being developed, map-learning as well as the traditional route-learning methods should be addressed to develop a more meaningful concept for students. Classroom teachers who utilize the 4 Ms in their teaching (meaningful material, motivation, movement, and multiple intelligences) are helping their students develop pride and self-worth by enabling them to see the relevance of what they are learning.

8

Valuing Honesty
and Ethics

In Chapter 1, we referred to the increase in violence and student aggression as a pertinent problem in our school system. Many incoming students seem to lack a basic understanding of appropriate values and good decision-making skills. Often, we see impulsive and inappropriate reactions from students who don't seem to know a more positive way of interacting. When proper morals aren't addressed or honored in the home, our job in the classroom becomes even more complicated. This chapter is intended to give classroom teachers some suggestions and activities to help students reflect on their ethics and determine whether they like what they see (see Figure 8.1).

As students mature and begin to develop their own sense of feelings, emotions, beliefs, and values, the issues of personal integrity and ethics become an important aspect of emotional intelligence. *Ethics* can be defined as a system of morals one chooses to abide by. By the time our students enter the first grade, they have had approximately six years in which to form a basis for responsibility, respect, cooperation, honesty, and integrity. This framework of ethics was shaped by their observations of their parents and siblings, as well as other environmental factors, such as influential adults, playmates, and the media. How can we, as teachers, help our students to obtain positive and productive ethics when so much has already been ingrained in them before they ever reach us?

In *An Integrated Approach to Character Education,* Timothy Rusnak (1998) describes six principles that develop stronger academic

FIGURE 8.1. Components of Emotional Intelligence

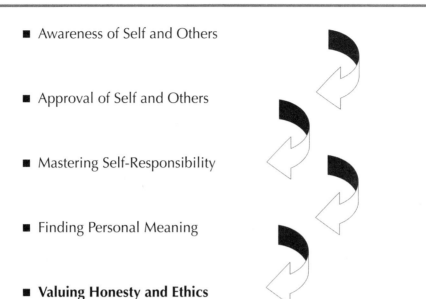

- Awareness of Self and Others

- Approval of Self and Others

- Mastering Self-Responsibility

- Finding Personal Meaning

- **Valuing Honesty and Ethics**

growth but that also focus on the social skills our students need to develop a stronger sense of ethics.

- *Character education as a part of every subject.* Although teachers have specific academic criteria in mind when they develop lesson plans, components of responsibility, respect, cooperation, hope, and determination should be integrated into each major lesson.

- *Going beyond discussion and simulation.* In implementing an ethics or character education program, it must be designed to progress toward the "morally mature person." This "action education" format must contain activities to reflect human dignity, to enhance nurturing and caring for the welfare of others, and to integrate individual interests with social responsibilities. It should also produce integrity, inspire moral choices, and involve resolution of conflict.

- *Positive school environment.* The entire school must be an environment of positive student support. The atmosphere must feel soothing yet challenging. The school procedures and policies must be clear and consistent. Teachers must be aware of their roles as leaders and models of ethical conduct. They must provide an environment that encourages student reflection and self-actualization.

■ *Administrative role in ethics education.* The role of administrators is to demonstrate and model the desired ethics just as teachers do. They must choose to include a character education program as an integral component of the curriculum and design benchmark standards with which to measure the success of the program.

■ *The empowered teacher in the ethics program.* This means that the teacher's role stretches way beyond that of information giver and curriculum manager. The teacher's role becomes one of decision maker, problem solver, and liaison. The teacher cooperates with parents and community and business partners to bring about a greater understanding in the students of the concepts of ethics and honesty.

■ *The school and community as crucial partners.* By linking students, teachers, parents, neighborhoods, community, and business leaders together, we provide the necessary components in an ethics education program. The integration of these components can take place through field trips to various community and business organizations, through pen pal projects, or through mentoring in the school. By maintaining relationships with outside entities, we embrace consistent and ethical role models in the classroom.

Parent Involvement

In addition to these six principles, a seventh component must be addressed—that of parental involvement. Without this component, our position in teaching ethics and honesty becomes next to impossible. For students to fully gain new ethical and honesty awareness and adjustments, parents must become a part of the school atmosphere. Parents who are available during the school day should be encouraged to take on the roles of classroom tutors or mentors, school volunteers, or field trip chaperones. Those who are not available throughout the day can show their support by responding to teacher notes and phone calls, checking student homework consistently, reading newsletters that go home, and having daily discussions with their children regarding events of the school day.

As educators, we can increase parental involvement by implementing a simple strategy. Make a list of all possible circumstances for which parental involvement is needed. Send the list home, or hand it to parents at the first parent conference. Let parents know that they are expected to sign up for one area in which they are willing to become involved. Your note might look similar to the one in Exhibit 8.1.

⚡ EXHIBIT 8.1

September 1, 20XX

Dear Parents,

We are looking forward to a rewarding and exciting year full of learning opportunities for your child. To ensure that your child has the very best education possible, I am asking parents to volunteer in one of the following areas. I feel that it is important that your child sees your interest in his or her education and appreciate your willingness to work as a team toward this goal.

Field trip chaperone _____   Grading papers _____

Tutor (in class) _____   Making phone calls _____

Office volunteer _____   Organizing events _____

Playground helper _____   Supervising lunch room _____

In addition, to show your interest in your child's learning, please make sure that you are reviewing homework with her or him and looking at graded papers. Also, please encourage your child to tell you about the events of our school day. Thank you for your support!

Sincerely,

Some schools feel so strongly about parental involvement that they have included it in the school policy book as an essential component of children's education. At Mingus Springs Charter School, a K through 8 school in Chino Valley, Arizona, parents are asked to donate 20 hours of volunteer time each school year. Volunteer options include making phone calls, tutoring in the classroom, correcting papers, building bookshelves, and working in the library. Parents keep track of their own hours of service in a logbook located in the school office. Parents who are not physically able to come to the school may help the school from home. School director Cathy O'Connell believes that for students to achieve true insight into ethics and integrity, role models, such as parents, must be visible and productive on the school campus.

Keeping in mind that emotional intelligence components are all linked together and should be taught in a sequence, honesty and ethics would be the last component in the chain. Even without this last step in the sequence, benefits achieved thus far would include the following abilities:

- Awareness of one's positive and negative attributes

- Approval and acceptance of oneself, flaws and all

- Recognition that one is responsible for one's actions, beliefs, and mistakes

- Finding personal meaning in academic, individual, and social events

Honesty and ethics are a natural way to bring the components of emotional intelligence full circle as a well-rounded individual emerges. Demonstrating character and good ethics are truly signs of maturity that result when a child has benefited from observing and interacting with positive adults and peers. Schools can foster the development of this final component by integrating self-awareness, self-approval, self-responsibility, and personal meaning into all subject areas. The implementation of programs that reflect human pride and dignity must be schoolwide rather than in only a few classrooms. The entire school must focus on the development of a calm and relaxing atmosphere in conjunction with stimulation and challenge. Administrators must support the integration of honesty and ethics into all subject areas and look for evidence of it as teachers are evaluated. Teachers should be encouraged to use modeling techniques for problem solving, decision making, and reflective thinking (metacognition). Intrinsic rather than extrinsic motivation and rewards should be emphasized as students try to achieve personal and academic goals. Career field trips, guest speakers, and mentors should serve as archetypes for students to demonstrate ethical and expected levels of job performance.

Through a schoolwide program that honors self-awareness, self-approval, self-responsibility, and personal meaning, honesty and ethics is a natural last link in the chain of emotional intelligence training.

The following activities are suggested for use with students to help them increase their honesty and ethics skills.

Honesty and Ethics Activity 1

JUST BECAUSE

Level: K through 8

Subject areas: Language Arts

Directions:
To practice the art of honesty and ethics, students brainstorm a list of all possible ideas to demonstrate the true meanings of these attributes.

Using an overhead projector or chalkboard, the teacher records the student-generated list of honesty and ethics activities. They are then asked to implement five of these ideas each day (just because!). Ideas for the student-generated list may include the following:

- Hold the door open for someone.

- If someone falls, help them up.

- If kids are laughing at someone, don't join in.

- If you make a mistake, admit it and learn from it.

- Compliment someone.

- Listen politely to others before voicing your opinion.

- Respect the opinions of others.

- Show respect for all types of people.

- Help a fellow student who doesn't understand an assignment.

Honesty and Ethics Activity 1

JUST BECAUSE

Level: K through 8

Subject areas: Language Arts

Directions:
After the students have generated a list of "Just Because" activities, they will then be asked to choose and implement five of these items each day for 1 week. They record the ethics activities they performed, and at the end of the week they reflect on their success in following through and their self-discoveries. (Very young students may share verbally.)

- Hold the door open for someone. _____
  _____

- If someone falls, help that person up. _____
  _____

- If kids are laughing at someone, don't join in. _____
  _____

- If you make a mistake, admit it and learn from it. _____
  _____

- Compliment someone. _____
  _____

- Listen politely to others before voicing your opinion. _____
  _____

- Respect the opinions of others. _____
  _____

- Show respect for all types of people. _____
  _____

- Help a fellow student who doesn't understand an assignment.
  _____

Honesty and Ethics Activity 1

JUST BECAUSE

Level: K through 8

Subject areas: Language Arts

Directions:
After implementing the new ethics and honesty behaviors for one week, students are asked to think about what they discovered about themselves by using this reflection sheet.
Kindergarten through 1st-grade students may share verbally.

1. Which "Just Because" items did you choose to implement this week?

2. Describe an incident in which you used a "Just Because" item.

3. Tell about your feelings during and after this incident.

Honesty and Ethics Activity 2

FABLE STUDIES

Level: K through 8

Subject areas: Language Arts

Directions:

During a study of fables, students analyze the various characters and list their ethical attributes (or lack of them). Next, students write a reflection of the fable character they most relate to and describe the similarities.

Kindergarten through 2nd-grade students may draw or discuss ethical attributes.

The Ant and the Grasshopper

In a field one summer's day, a Grasshopper was hopping about, chirping and singing to its heart's content. An Ant passed by, bearing along with great toil an ear of corn he was taking to the nest.

Grasshopper: Why not come and chat with me, instead of toiling and moiling in that way?

Ant: I am helping to lay up food for the winter, and I recommend you to do the same.

Grasshopper: Why bother about winter? We have got plenty of food at present.

But the Ant went on its way and continued its toil. When the winter came, the Grasshopper had no food and found itself dying of hunger, while it saw the ants distributing every day corn and grain from the stores they had collected in the summer. Then the Grasshopper knew:
It is best to prepare for the days of necessity.

—*Aesop's Fables*

Honesty and Ethics Activity 2

FABLE STUDIES

Level: K through 8

Subject areas: Language Arts

Directions:

During a study of fables, students analyze the various characters and list their ethical attributes (or lack of them). Next, students write a reflection of the fable character they most relate to and describe the similarities.

Kindergarten through 2nd-grade students may draw or discuss ethical attributes.

The Lion and the Mouse

Once when a Lion was asleep, a little Mouse began running up and down upon him; this soon awakened the Lion, who placed his huge paw upon him, and opened his big jaws to swallow him.

Mouse: Pardon, O King, forgive me this time, I shall never forget it; who knows but what I may be able to do you a turn some of these days?

The Lion was so tickled at the idea of the Mouse being able to help him that he lifted up his paw and let him go. Some time after, the Lion was caught in a trap, and the hunters who desired to carry him alive to the King tied him to a tree while they went in search of a wagon to carry him on. Just then the little Mouse happened to pass by and seeing the sad plight in which the Lion was, went up to him and soon gnawed away the ropes that bound the King of the Beasts. "Was I not right?" said the little Mouse.
    Little friends may prove great friends.

—Aesop's Fables

Honesty and Ethics Activity 3

FINISH MY FABLE

Level: 3 through 8

Subject areas: Language Arts

Directions:

Using blank comic strip frames, Student 1 draws and writes the first half of the comic strip fable. Student 1 should stop at the frame where the problem has arisen. Student 1 passes the half-finished comic strip fable to Student 2. This student has the job of finishing the comic strip frames and the fable. When it is completed, Student 1 and Student 2 get back together and decide on a moral of the story. When all class members are finished with the project, they share orally their comic strip fables and morals. The following comic frame can be used for this project.

Title: _____

Moral: _____

_____

_____

PART III

Incorporating Emotional Intelligence Into the Curriculum

EI Synthesis: Creating a Thematic Unit Around Emotional Intelligence

This chapter is intended to "bring it all together" for the teacher. The process of implementing an emotional intelligence program in a classroom is covered step by step. Pre- and postassessments are included for teachers' use, and finally, a prepared thematic unit with emotional intelligence components integrated into the lessons is shared (see Figure 9.1).

Step-by-Step Implementation

Although fostering emotional intelligence should be a daily, ongoing process, the thought of instituting all of the emotional intelligence components may seem overwhelming at first. By following these steps in the first couple of months of the school year, teachers can feel confident that their students will gain academic, social, and emotional benefits from the new program. If you teach in a district that does not value or understand the importance of emotional intelligence, feel free to pick and choose from this list—a little insight is better than no insight. Perhaps when others see the postassessments of your students, they will acknowledge the value of this program.

FIGURE 9.1. Components of Emotional Intelligence: Putting Them All Together

- ■ **Awareness of Self and Others**

- ■ **Approval of Self and Others**

- ■ **Mastering Self-Responsibility**

- ■ **Finding Personal Meaning**

- ■ **Valuing Honesty and Ethics**

- ■ Before the school year starts, take a look around your classroom. Is it physically inviting and warm? Is it set up to be challenging, yet relaxing (relaxed alertness)?

- ■ As you meet your students, look each one in the eye and shake his or her hand. Let them see that each one of them is important to you. Be observant of personal hygiene, aggressive tendencies, or signs of violence in the home.

- ■ Use the "What Does Emotional Intelligence Look Like?" chart from Chapter 1 and "Emotional Intelligence Needs Checklist" from Chapter 2 to do a quick overall assessment of your students.

- ■ With student input, create a No Fear plan (see Chapter 2).

- ■ With student input, create a learning definition (see Chapter 2).

- ■ After you have been acquainted with your students for several weeks, administer the formal preassessment to each student and for each emotional intelligence component. Graph the results for each student and the overall class averages.

- ■ Students who have unusually low scores in any area should be monitored by you, a school counselor, or school nurse.

- ■ Begin instituting emotional intelligence activities that focus on peer relations by having students complete the Relationship

Self-Assessment (Table 3.1) and Relationship Attributes in other students (Table 3.2). After they complete these checklists, complete written reflections and discussion activities.

- Implement violence prevention lessons (see Chapter 3).

- Discuss cognizant awareness with students and integrate awareness activities into content lessons (see Chapter 4).

- Discuss approval of self and others and integrate approval activities into content lessons (see Chapter 5).

- Discuss the methods of mastering self-responsibility and integrate activities into content lessons (see Chapter 6).

- Discuss the importance of finding personal meaning in learning and integrate activities into content lessons (see Chapter 7).

- Discuss the lifelong benefits of honesty and ethics and integrate activities into content lessons (see Chapter 8).

- Throughout the school year, lessons should include components that trigger an emotional response, such as debates, editorials, group presentations, personal interest projects, and so on.

- Throughout the school year, students should have plenty of time to reflect on their academic, social, and emotional well-being. This reflection process may take the form of journal writing, class discussion, peer sharing, or cooperative group strategies.

- Toward the end of the school year, teachers should once again assess the emotional intelligence of their students by using the postassessment. Again, graph individual results for each emotional intelligence component; then graph the class averages.

- Make note of any success. Teachers in schools using portfolio assessments should pass this assessment to the student's next teacher.

Once the school year is underway and teachers have gained an understanding of their students, an emotional intelligence assessment based on teacher observation should be given. The Assessment Appendix on pages 133-141 includes a rubric for teachers to use as they assess current levels of individual students' emotional intelligence. Next are the assessment sheets for each of the emotional intelligence components (i.e., self-awareness, self-approval, self-responsibility, personal meaning, and honesty and ethics). Each student should be assessed on these attributes at the beginning of the school year and again at the end of the year to determine emotional intelligence growth. Also included is an individual student assessment graph and a class average emotional intelligence graph. The individual assessment graph may become a part of a portfolio or student record to be passed to the next teacher.

Educators should use the graphed information to determine how successful the integration of emotional intelligence into content areas has been. Comparisons of individual student assessments from the beginning and the end of a school year should be examined as well as entire class average emotional intelligence scores. This information can then be used to restructure or modify the school's emotional intelligence program.

Revolutionary War: A Thematic Unit

The following thematic unit has been developed to demonstrate the effective incorporation of emotional intelligence attributes into a content unit for 5th- through 8th-grade students.

1765:	The Stamp Act; repealed in 1766
March 5, 1770:	The Boston Massacre
December 16, 1773:	The Boston Tea Party
September 1774:	First Continental Congress Meets in Philadelphia
April 19, 1775:	Gage seizes military supplies at Concord. Battle of Lexington
May 10, 1775:	Second Continental Congress Meets in Philadelphia
May 10, 1775:	Capture by colonists of forts and arsenals at Ticonderoga
May 11, 1775:	Battle of Crown Point; victory for the Green Mountain Boys
June 15, 1775:	Washington appointed Commander-in-Chief by Congress
June 17, 1775:	Battle of Bunker Hill; British occupy Boston until March 1776
December 31, 1775:	Expedition to Canada fails; Benedict Arnold wounded
July 4, 1776:	Declaration of Independence signed; United Colonies become the United States of America, each colony becomes a state
August 1776:	Arrival of 30,000 British troops in New York harbor
August 27, 1776:	Battle of Long Island; Americans defeated
September 16, 1776:	Battle of Harlem Heights; Americans defeated
October 28, 1776:	Battle of White Plains; Americans defeated
December 25, 1776 to January 3, 1777:	Crossing of the Delaware and Battles of Trenton and Princeton. Brilliant American victories
July 5, 1777:	Ticonderoga captured by the British
September 19 to October 7, 1777:	Battle of Saratoga; American victory
October 17, 1777:	Burgoyne surrenders his entire army to the Americans
September 11, 1777:	Battle of Brandywine; Americans defeated

October 4, 1777:   Battle of Germantown; Americans retreat with near victory

June 28, 1778:   Battle of Monmouth; British retire under cover of night

December 29, 1778:   Savannah taken by the British

1779:   Lafayette goes to France to plead for help

September 1779:   John Paul Jones captures man-of-war near English coast

May 12, 1780:   Charlestown, South Carolina, taken by the British

August 16, 1780:   Gates defeated by Cornwallis near Camden, South Carolina

September 23, 1780:   Benedict Arnold's plot to surrender West Point frustrated

October 7, 1780:   Battle of King's Mountain; British defeated

1780:   Rochambeau arrives in America with 5,500 men

1781:   Powerful French fleet under deGrasse arrives

March 15, 1781:   Battle of Guilford Court House; Americans defeated, but a costly victory for British

1781:   Greene clears interior of South Carolina and Georgia of the enemy

October 19, 1781:   Cornwallis trapped at Yorktown; he surrenders

November 30, 1782:   Provisional peace

September 3, 1783:   Treaty of Peace of Paris

Before the Unit

Before the unit begins, take the following steps in preparation:

- Gather Revolutionary War library books, Internet sources, videos, plays, literature studies, and so on for student use.

- Decide on the curriculum objectives that need to be addressed during the unit.

- Make a timeline going around the room using the above dates and information. Fill in some of the information, but leave some blanks to be filled in as the unit progresses.

- Make a display table for art supplies, Revolutionary War pictures and posters, and resource information for student use.

■ Outline the unit by creating 10 substantial assignments to be posted on a "Countdown Board." These 10 projects are to be worked on at the end of every lesson. Quizzes and other short assignments will be filled in later. To decide on your 10 major project assignments, use the outline in Table 9.1.

TABLE 9.1 Revolutionary War Unit and Emotional Intelligence Integration

Subject	Lesson Objective	Emotional Intelligence Integration
Reading/Language Arts/ Social Studies	Students will gain background information about the American Revolution by reading *My Brother Sam Is Dead* as a literature study. Student spelling words will be taken from this story.	As students read this book, they will discuss the feelings and emotions that these characters are feeling. In their journals, they will begin a list of adjectives to describe the integrity and emotions of the characters.
Writing/Language Arts/ Social Studies	Students will put themselves in the place of a colonist who has made his or her home in America. They will write a letter to relatives in England describing the undercurrent of emotions between the English and colonists.	As students gather information in the prewriting stage, they will be developing awareness and approval attributes because they will have to be understanding of opposing viewpoints.
History/Science	Students will compare the technology, building and housing construction, and creature comforts between England in the 1700s and America in the 1700s. They will make a diorama or other model type to show some of these differences.	Because this is an independent project with a due date, students will be practicing self-responsibility in task completion and will search for personal meaning in this project.
Math/Social Studies	After reading various materials about the Revolution, students will form partner teams and make a timeline showing 10 of the most crucial events that led to the American Revolution.	Students will be involved in decision making, cooperative skills, and problem solving with their partners because they must narrow down their list to only the 10 most crucial pre-Revolution events.
Science/Social Studies	The mission: In cooperative groups, students determine who really did fire the first shot at Lexington. Each member of the group will research a certain aspect of this problem.	Students will be developing self-responsibility as well as ethics and integrity because they will all be responsible for a certain piece of the puzzle. This fosters interdependence and group cohesion.

(continued)

TABLE 9.1 Continued

Subject	Lesson Objective	Emotional Intelligence Integration
Math/Social Studies	Students will chart the major battles of the Revolution with the number of casualties in each. They will make a graph of the casualties for comparison and contrast.	Based on the numbers of casualties, students will determine if freedom was worth the price they paid. Open class discussion format and individual journaling are called for.
Language Arts/Social Studies	Class debate: Some students will take on the role of colonists and some will be British representatives. At a mock town meeting, they will debate the right for American freedom.	After this debate takes place, students should have a discussion about how they felt as someone from the opposing side spoke harshly to them. Discuss the reasons behind the tense emotions. Have students write about a time in their own life when they felt this threatened.
All subjects	Students will choose an independent project to demonstrate their knowledge of the American Revolution. They may compose a song, make a replica of a battle, research a famous person from this era, or create artifacts from this time period.	Students should find relaxed alertness with this project because they will be stimulated yet not threatened by this assignment. The goal would also be achieving personal meaning and relevant learning.
Drama/Language Arts/ Social Studies	In teams of four, students will choose a famous event, such as the Boston Tea Party. They will create a written script and then perform the skit for the class.	Students, by now, will have developed awareness and acceptance for both sides of this issue. The skit will reinforce the feelings and emotions behind the actions taken.
All subjects: Culminating presentation	Students now have nine major assignments that they will display on poster board. They will present their projects to the class in a formal presentation.	Students will gain a sense of pride as they display all their projects and explain them to the class. Also, when students know that they will have this presentation opportunity at the end of each unit, they will want to do their best work. Parents should be invited and involved in this culminating event.

Starting the Unit

As an introduction to the Revolutionary War unit, show a video clip from the Walt Disney movie *Johnny Tremain*. This movie gives students a feel for the customs, clothing, weapons, culture, and so on of the 1700s. Then, work with your students on the following items:

- During this introductory video, ask students to write down five W questions (who, what, when, where, why). Discuss these questions at the end of the video.

- Ask students to ponder this thought:

  When a child is young, his parents take care of him, keep him safe, and make all of the decisions for him. As he grows and matures, he begins to need some freedom to solve his own problems and make decisions on his own. He develops his own opinions and has outgrown the need for parental control.

- Now, keeping the *Johnny Tremain* video in mind, write a few paragraphs in your journal about the connection between this boy and the American colonists.

- Ask students to think about a time when they needed to exert their independence (drawing on prior knowledge).

- Present the thematic bulletin board to students, which shows the major assignments with their due dates. Your thematic board might look something similar to this:

COUNTDOWN ACTIVITIES

10. *My Brother Sam Is Dead*
    Due: April 20

9. Colonist Letter
   Due: April 25

8. England/America: 1700s
   Due: May 1

7. Revolutionary Timeline
   Due: May 5

6. Who Fired the First Shot???
   Due: May 13

5. Charting the Battles
   Due: May 18

4. Class Debate
   Due: May 23

3. Independent Project
   Due: May 25

2. A Revolutionary Skit
   Due: May 30

1. Culminating Presentation
   Due: June 2

The Ongoing Unit

Students are given opportunities to work on the Countdown Board activities at the end of each lesson. The three sample lessons for this unit that follow may also provide guidance.

LESSON 1: READING TO GAIN EMPATHY

Students are presented with an excerpt that demonstrates the emotional impact of the Revolutionary War on the rebel and loyalist soldiers and colonists. The overall lesson objective is to help students gain empathy and understanding through reading comprehension.

1. Students are asked to think about a time when they were very sick or uncomfortable and away from home.

2. Students preview the written or visual excerpt silently.

3. In groups of four, students decide on vocabulary words from the excerpt that they need to define to fully understand the feelings and emotions of the soldiers and colonists.

4. In groups, students define these words and then further discuss the excerpt. They underline passages that evoke emotions or feelings.

5. Each group orally shares the underlined passages and explains why they found the passages emotionally touching.

6. Students volunteer to read orally certain passages with feeling.

7. At the end of the lesson, students work independently on their countdown projects.

Literature Resources for Excerpt Use

Forbes, Esther. (1968). *Johnny Tremain*. New York: Dell.

> *Johnny Tremain* is a classic piece of literature about a young apprentice silversmith who becomes involved in the events prior to the Revolutionary War, such as the Boston Tea Party. This historical fiction story lets the reader feel the excitement of breaking free from England, as well as the emotional and physical trauma of war.

Gregory, Kristiana. (1996). *The Winter of Red Snow: The Revolutionary War Diary of Abigail Jane Stewart*. New York: Scholastic (Dear America Series).

This historical fiction book is an emotionally descriptive diary of an 11-year-old girl in 1777. The first-person diary format allows students to gain empathy for the hardships and suffering that soldiers and colonists endured during the Revolution.

Hallahan, William H. (2000). *The Day the American Revolution Began: 19 April 1775*. New York: William Morrow.

This authentic and detailed account describes the Lexington and Concord battles in detail. Hallahan uses diaries, letters, official documents, and memoirs to bring the colonists' feelings and passions alive in the minds of readers.

Langguth, A. J. (1989). *Patriots: The Men Who Started the American Revolution*. New York: Simon & Schuster.

This narrative helps students develop insight into the emotional intelligence of the key men who instigated the fight for freedom. Heroes such as George Washington, John Adams, Samuel Adams, Ben Franklin, and Patrick Henry are highlighted.

Leckie, Robert. (1993). *George Washington's War: The Saga of the American Revolution*. New York: Harper Trade.

This selection is unique in that viewpoints, motives, and behaviors of both British and American leadership are portrayed. The ugliness and chaos of various battles are described as well as the betrayals of traitors such as Charles Lee and Benedict Arnold.

From the Diary of Albigence Waldo, Surgeon at Valley Forge, 1777. From Revolution to Reconstruction: A WWW project in collective writing [online]. Available at: http://odur.let.rug.nl/~usa/D/1776-1800/war/waldo.htm

Albigence Waldo was a surgeon during the Revolutionary War and his diary describes the agony and emotional pain of wounded and dying soldiers as well as the loneliness, hunger, and cold that the soldiers had to endure. This excerpt provides many opportunities for empathy discussions.

LESSON 2: FINDING MEANING THROUGH GREAT LEADERS

The objective of this lesson is to analyze quotations of Samuel Adams, American patriot. Students, who would now have some background knowledge of the Revolution, gain deep meaning because of their prior knowledge.

1. Read background information about Samuel Adams.

2. Read famous Samuel Adams quotations orally.

3. Each team of four students is given a quotation to explore. Teams use resource materials, dictionaries, and so on to gain full understanding of the quotation.

4. Each team shares orally what their quotation means.

5. Based on the quotations and background information given, students write a character sketch of Samuel Adams. This sketch should include the following factors:

   - His physical, social, and emotional abilities

   - His cognitive self-awareness level

   - His self-approval level

   - His level of responsibility

   - His ethics and honesty

   - His deep understanding of meaning (with regard to the cause of the American Revolutionary War)

6. Students work on their countdown projects on completion of this lesson.

LESSON 3: PLOTTING FAMOUS BATTLES

Students become more aware and accepting of the affected areas of the United States during the American Revolution. Each student is given a United States map as our country looked in 1775. Using resource material and group interaction, students locate and plot the 1775 battles and places of major action during the Revolution. To create an atmosphere of self-responsibility, students could work on this in pairs. Each partner would be responsible for the location and plotting of half the events.

Dates and Locations of Events of the American Revolution

April 19, 1775, Lexington, Massachusetts

April 19, 1775, Concord, Massachusetts

May 5, 1775, Martha's Vineyard, Massachusetts

May 10, 1775, Ticonderoga, New York

May 12, 1775, Crown Point, New York

May 14, 1775, Fort St. John, Canada

May 21, 1775, Grape Island, Massachusetts

May 27, 1775, Hogg Island, Massachusetts

June 17, 1775, Bunker Hill (Breed's Hill), Masschusetts

June 17, 1775, to March 17, 1776, Boston, Masschusetts

July 8, 1775, Roxbury, Masschusetts

August 13, 1775, Gloucester, Massachusetts

August 29, 1775, New York City

September 18, 1775, St. Johns, Canada

September 25, 1775, Montreal, Canada

September 30, 1775, Stonington, Connecticut

October 7, 1775, Bristol, Rhode Island

October 18, 1775, Falmouth, Maine

October 19, 1775, Chambly, Canada

October 26, 1775, Hampton, Virginia

November 3, 1775, St. Johns, Canada

November 9, 1775, Phipps's Farm, Masschusetts

November 12, 1775, Montreal, Canada

November 14, 1775, Kemp's Landing, Virgina

November 19 and 21, 1775, Ninety-Six, South Carolina

November 8-31, 1775, Quebec, Canada

December 9, 1775, Great Bridge, Virginia

December 22, 1775, Cane Brake, South Carolina

December 31, 1775, Quebec, Canada

Concluding the Unit

Near the end of the unit, students should have received feedback on their countdown projects. All the final draft projects now can be exhibited on a display board. Students rehearse a presentation that includes the following elements:

- Brief explanation of all projects

- Personal feelings about project that were most significant in the learner's opinion

- Three Revolutionary War events that had the greatest impact on this learner

This type of presentation is a performance-based assessment. Rather than a formal multiple-choice or essay test, this presentation would be the final assessment about the material covered. Providing students with the opportunity to present their projects and explain their personal feelings about the learning means they will obtain much deeper meaning and long-term memory of the subject.

Revolutionary War Unit Teacher References

Books

Brash, S. (Ed.). (1998). *War Between Brothers.* New York: Time-Life.
Moore, K. (1998). *If You Had Lived at the Time of the American Revolution.* New York: Scholastic.

DVD and VHS

The Revolutionary War (1993). Simitar Video.

Audiocassette

McNeil, R. (1989). *American History Through Folksong With Historical Narration.* Riverside, CA: WEM Records.

World Wide Web

http://www.looksmart.com
http://www.geocities.com/Heartland/Ranch/9198/revwar/concord.htm
http://encarta.msn.com/find/Concise.asp?ti=027BE000

Appendix

Pre- and Post-Training Assessment of Emotional Intelligence

Scoring Rubric

Directions:

The emotional intelligence assessment is based on the teacher's observation. It should not be given until after the school year is underway, when teachers have gained an ample understanding of their students. Each student is assessed on each of the five emotional intelligence components. A graph is filled out for each student along with a graph showing the overall class rating. As you score the emotional intelligence of students, use the following rubric:

0 = Student exhibits no understanding or use of this skill.

1 = Student exhibits very little understanding or use of this skill.

2 = Student exhibits some understanding or use of this skill.

3 = Student exhibits moderate understanding or use of this skill.

4 = Student exhibits extensive understanding or use of this skill.

5 = Student exhibits a mastery level understanding and use of this skill.

Assessment 1

Cognizant Awareness of Self and Others

Directions:

Use the rubric on page 143 to score each student on the following awareness attributes.

Rate each student's awareness regarding the following factors:

_____ 1. Physical self (appearance and reaction of others to appearance)

_____ 2. Academic strengths and weakness of self and others

_____ 3. Social strengths and weaknesses of self and peers

_____ 4. Personal interests and taste in music, art, and so on

_____ 5. His or her own feelings and emotions

_____ 6. Feelings and emotions of others

_____ 7. His or her own appropriate and inappropriate responses to emotional triggers

_____ 8. Appropriate or inappropriate responses of others to emotional triggers

_____ 9. Why he or she is feeling what she or he is feeling

_____ 10. His or her own beliefs, attitudes, and values

Assessment 2

Approval of Self and Others

Directions:

Use the rubric on page 143 to score each student on the following approval attributes.

Rate each student's approval or acceptance level regarding the following factors:

_____ 1. Physical self-attributes

_____ 2. Academic strengths and weaknesses

_____ 3. Current social status with peers

_____ 4. His or her own feelings and emotions

_____ 5. Feelings and emotions of others

_____ 6. His or her own values, beliefs, attitudes, and opinions

_____ 7. Values, beliefs, attitudes, and opinions of others

_____ 8. Optimistic strategies in academic or social situations

_____ 9. Self-acceptance in general

_____ 10. Acceptance level in general regarding peers

Assessment 3

Mastering Self-Responsibility

Directions:

Use the rubric on page 143 to score each student on the following self-responsibility attributes.

Rate each student's responsibility level regarding the following factors:

_____ 1. Instant gratification impulses

_____ 2. Concern for feelings of others

_____ 3. Time management skills

_____ 4. School preparation and homework assignments

_____ 5. Effective, assertive language skills (vs. passive or aggressive)

_____ 6. Neatness and organizational skills

_____ 7. Problem-solving skills

_____ 8. Action and behavior control

_____ 9. Natural consequences for actions of self and others

_____ 10. Thought processes that lead to appropriate choices

Assessment 4

Finding Personal Meaning

Directions:

Use the rubric on page 143 to score each student on the following personal meaning attributes.

Rate each student's personal meaning level regarding the following factors:

_____ 1. Interest in thematic topics

_____ 2. Class discussions

_____ 3. Parent involvement in school (through phone calls, notes, volunteer time, field trips, etc.)

_____ 4. Involvement in independent studies

_____ 5. Engagement in a variety of learning experiences

_____ 6. Relationship between new information and prior knowledge

_____ 7. Intrinsic motivation to learn

_____ 8. Metacognitive processing (thinks about the learning and how he or she feels about it)

_____ 9. Involvement with cooperative learning activities

_____ 10. Insight and reflection with regard to academic, social, and emotional events

Assessment 5

Valuing Honesty and Ethics

Directions:

Use the rubric on page 143 to score each student on the following honesty and ethics attributes.

Rate each student's honesty and ethics level regarding the following factors:

_____ 1. Respect for those in authority

_____ 2. Responsibility in and follow-through with task completion

_____ 3. Cooperation skills with peers and adults

_____ 4. Honesty on a day-to-day basis

_____ 5. Ability to accept blame after making a poor decision

_____ 6. Ability to voice opinions in an appropriate way

_____ 7. Determination and motivation in schoolwork and extra-curricular activities

_____ 8. Problem situations and formulating an appropriate plan of action

_____ 9. Parent involvement in student's school life (through phone calls, notes, volunteering, etc.)

_____ 10. Interest in and concern for the well-being of others

Individual Student Assessment Graph

Student Name: _____

Directions:

Teachers should have the pre- and postassessment scores based on the scoring rubric on page 143.

For each assessment, add up the rubric points and divide the total by 10. For example, if a student received a rubric score of 5 for each of the 10 attributes in the Cognizant Awareness pretest, the total number of points would be 50. This score divided by 10 would be 5. The bar graph would be colored from 0-5, which would demonstrate the highest score possible for the Cognizant Awareness attribute. Color in the bar graphs to show student emotional intelligence status.

5					
4					
3					
2					
1					
0					
	Cognizant Awareness	*Approval of Self & Others*	*Self-Responsibility*	*Personal Meaning*	*Ethics & Honesty*

The average emotional intelligence score for this student is _____.
To determine the overall average emotional intelligence score, add up all points and divide by five. Use this information for the Class Average Worksheet on page 150.

Teacher comments:

_____

_____

_____

Class Emotional Intelligence Assessment Average

Directions:

Use individual average scores to fill in the class average scores for emotional intelligence.

Student Names	Average Emotional Intelligence Scores				
	1	2	3	4	5

Afterword

We can no longer assume that our job as educators is only to instill solid academic learning within our students. Certainly, student skill development is our main focus, but with societal changes, stability of the home deteriorating, and student stress levels increasing, our role as educators must take on a whole new function. We must now incorporate values, morals, empathy, and self-awareness attributes into our daily lessons. We must see to it our students are not only aware of how they deal with issues but of why they deal with them in the way they do. We must teach them to question themselves regarding their reactions. Students must be trained to observe the actions of others and ponder the causes and appropriateness of the actions.

In light of school violence and emotional impulses that are out of control, we can no longer bury our heads in the sand and insist our job is to "teach," not to parent. Bear in mind that research suggests the trait of aggression often stems from parent neglect or abuse. If parents are not equipped to do the parenting, then it must fall to someone else. Yes, we do have a full curriculum, and yes, our hands are already full from the demands of administrators, parents, and students. But with careful planning, emotional intelligence activities can easily become a part of the everyday curriculum.

Emotional intelligence components are not difficult to integrate and can be as simple as looking students in the eye and letting them know you care. My suggestion is to follow the steps of integration outlined in the last chapter. If some of the steps are not feasible for you currently, then by all means, leave them out! It's better to incorporate some emotional intelligence strategies than none at all.

Remember that emotional intelligence is not "just one more thing you have to teach." It is not a subject or an isolated skill one can teach. It is the process of learning to understand our own emotions, learning to understand the emotions of others, gaining proficiency in positive emotional responses, and recognizing and accepting emotional responses of others.

By integrating relevant teaching strategies that invoke meaningful learning on the part of students, we can help students gain insight into their own emotional intelligence. As the emotional understanding of an individual goes up, so does academic performance, improved social skills, problem-solving ability, and self-worth.

Through incorporation of emotional intelligence components, students' perception of self as well as an understanding of emotions in others can be obtained; this is the first step for our students in gaining the essential skills for a well-rounded and successful life.

Our students will someday be the voice of this country, its decision makers, and motivators. Let's give them the opportunity to make a meaningful impact on life. Let's give them the tools necessary to cooperate, influence, perceive, and promote positive change. Let's create emotionally intelligent leaders.

References

Asher, S., & Williams, G. (1987). Helping children without friends in home and school contexts. In *Children's social development: Information for parents and teachers.* Urbana: University of Illinois Press.

Bennett, E. L., Diamond, M. C., Krech, D., & Rozenzweig, M. R. (1964). Chemical and anatomical plasticity of the brain. *Science, 146,* 610-619.

Branden, N. (1994). *The six pillars of self-esteem.* New York: Bantam.

Caine, G., & Caine, R. N. (1994). *Making connections: Teaching and the human brain.* Menlo Park, CA: Addison-Wesley.

Etzioni, A., Berkowitz, M. C., & Wilcox, W. B. (1995). *Character building for a democratic, civil society.* Position paper for the Communitarian Network. (Available from the Communitarian Network, 2130 H Street, NW, Suite 703, Washington, DC 20052; 1-800-245-7460; http://gwis.circ.gwu.edu/~ccps/)

Gardner, H. (1993). *Multiple intelligences: The theory in practice.* New York: Basic Books.

Goleman, D. (1997). *Emotional intelligence: Why it can matter more than IQ.* New York: Bantam.

Hannaford, C. (1995). *Smart moves: Why learning is not all in your head.* Arlington, VA: Great Ocean.

Haynes, N. M., Comer, J. P., & Hamilton-Lee, M. (1988). The school development program: A model for school improvement. *Journal of Negro Education, 57,* 11-21.

Henry, T. (1995, February 21). Student grades count for little with employers. *USA Today,* D-1.

Huesmann, L. R., Eron, L. D., & Warnicke-Yarmel, P. W. (1987). Intellectual functioning and aggression. *Journal of Personality and Social Psychology, 52,* 232-240.

Katz, L. G. (1985). Dispositions in Early Childhood Education. *ERIC/EECE Bulletin, 18*(2), 1-3.

Mackenzie, R. (1996). *Setting limits in the classroom.* Rockland, CA: Prima.

153

Martin, L. (1991). *What work requires of schools.* Secretary's Commission on Acquiring Necessary Skills (SCANS). Retrieved January 10, 2001 from the World Wide Web: www.scans.jhu.edu/General/workreq.html

Nowicki, S., & Duke, M. (1989, August). A measure of nonverbal social processing ability in children between the ages of 6 and 10. Paper presented at the American Psychological Society, New Orleans, LA.

Olson, L. (1997). *The school-to-work revolution.* Reading, MA: Perseus.

Purkey, W. (1988). *An overview of self-concept theory for counselors.* Ann Arbor, MI: ERIC Clearinghouse on Counseling and Personal Services.

Rusnak, T. (1998). *An integrated approach to character education.* Thousand Oaks, CA: Corwin.

Slovey, P., & Mayer, J. D. (1990). Emotional intelligence. *Imagination, Cognition, and Personality, 9,* 185-211.

Sperry, R. (1974). *Lateral specialization in the surgically separated hemispheres* (Neurosciences Third Study Program). Cambridge: MIT Press.

Additional Resources

Bodine, R. J., Crawford, D. K., & Schrumpf, F. (1995). *Creating the peaceable school: A comprehensive program for teaching conflict resolution*. Champaign, IL: Research Press.

Fogarty, R. (1997). *Problem-based learning & other curriculum models*. Arlington Heights, IL: Skylight Training and Publishing.

Quinn, M. M., Bable, R. A., Rutherford, R. B., Nelson, C. M., & Howell, K. W. (1998). *Addressing student problem behavior: An IEP team's introduction to functional behavioral assessment and behavior intervention plans*. Washington DC: American Institutes for Research, Center for Effective Collaboration and Practice.

CORWIN
PRESS

The Corwin Press logo—a raven striding across an open book—represents the happy union of courage and learning. We are a professional-level publisher of books and journals for K–12 educators, and we are committed to creating and providing resources that embody these qualities. Corwin's motto is "Success for All Learners."